The Romberg Sonata in C Major

Study Book

for Cello

Exercises by Cassia Harvey
Sonata by Bernhard Romberg
with edits by F. Jansen

CHP348

©2018 by C. Harvey Publications All Rights Reserved.

www.learnstrings.com - downloadable books
www.charveypublications.com - print books

The Romberg Sonata in C Major Study Book for Cello

Table of Contents

Movement One (Allegro) Exercises	**Page**
Part One (measures 1-16)	3
Part Two (measures 17-28)	8
Part Three (measures 29-48)	12
Part Four (measures 49-69)	16
Part Five (measures 70-80a)	20
Part Six (measures 80-91)	29
Part Seven (measures 92-112)	33
Part Eight (measures 113-128)	38
Part Nine (measures 129-141a)	43
Part Ten (measures 141-158)	48
Part Eleven (measures 159-166)	54
Part Twelve (measures 167-186; end)	59

Movement Two (Andante) Exercises	**Page**
Part One (measures 1-12)	67
Part Two (measures 13-27)	70
Part Three (measures 28-36)	76
Part Four (measures 37-49)	82
Part Five (measures 50-59)	83

Movement Three (Allegretto) Exercises	**Page**
Essential Bowing Exercises	88
Part One (measures 1-16)	93
Part Two (measures 17-28)	96
Part Three (measures 29-48)	102
Part Four (measures 49-69)	106
Part Five (measures 70-80a)	108
Part Six (measures 80-91)	113
Part Seven (measures 92-112)	117
Part Eight (measures 113-128)	121

Complete Sonata	**Page**
Allegro	128
Andante	132
Allegretto	134

©2018 C. Harvey Publications All Rights Reserved.

How this book works

This book divides *Sonata in C Major*, by Bernhard Romberg, into short sections and provides exercises for mastering each section.

Each exercise was written to teach a specific skill. **Shifts** are often repeated to help with acquiring muscle memory. **Double stops** are included for establishing relative pitch, building left-hand strength, and balancing the bow across two strings. Most of the bowing work focuses on the various slur and articulation combinations that Romberg includes in his piece. Rhythm is often taught by subdividing longer notes into shorter beats.

Vibrato may be used throughout the book as soon as intonation is secure. Playing the exercises with vibrato will help balance the hand over the notes being played and will also help develop tone.

Metronome markings are suggestions. The slower tempo can be used after you have just learned the notes and are ready to work on the rhythm. Every time you play the exercise, you can move a few notches or numbers faster on the metronome until you reach the faster tempo listed. Feel free to play slower or faster than the listed metronome markings so that the exercises are the most helpful for you.

In exercises where no metronome indications are given, start slowly to learn the notes. When you repeat the exercise, increase your speed until you are close to the tempo of the *Sonata*.

Roman numerals refer to strings (never positions).
I = A string
II = D string
III = G string
IV = C string

Spiccato and Staccato in Romberg's Sonata in C Major

Staccato is a short, sharp bow-stroke where the bow remains on the string.

Staccato is used in the exercises to develop good tone, even bow speed, and a controlled bow technique. In these cases, listen for a clearly articulated sound and stop the bow completely at the end of the note.

Spiccato is a controlled bouncing stroke where the bow comes off the string.

Romberg included many instances of spiccato bowing in this Sonata, however there is no rule for how much the bow needs to come up off the string. In many cases, I play these spiccato notes as just slightly detached and barely off the string; more of a leggiero. The effect of these notes is to make the music light and **it is more important to focus on the lightness of sound than on having a bow that bounces high off the string**.

The amount of lift in the bow is left to the discretion of the performer. The bow might even be kept on the string, if played lightly.

In his method, Romberg writes: "In making the stroke, not more than a finger's breadth of the length of the bow should be used. The motion of the bow is here made entirely with the hand, and with not too great a pressure. The arm, as usual, must be held free from all stiffness."

Some preparatory books and pieces to study before or along with this book:

Fourth Position for the Cello *or* Fourth Position Study Method for the Cello

Second Position for the Cello

Third Position for the Cello

Fifth Position Preparatory Studies for the Cello

Fifth Position for the Cello

The C Major Scale Book for Cello

Bowing Variations for the Cello, Book One

String Crossing for the Cello, Book Two

The Bach Cello Suite No. 1 Study Book

The Romberg Sonata in E minor for Cello and Piano

Some books and pieces to study after this book:

Tenor Clef for the Cello

Arpeggio Studies in Two Octaves for the Cello

The D Major Scale Book for Cello

Goltermann Concerto No. 4 for Cello and Piano

Tarantella by Squire

The Swan Study Book for Cello

For a free copy of *The Romberg Sonata in C Major Practice Edition*, with the complete Sonata as a duet, visit www.charveypublications.com/rombergcmajorpractice.

©2018 C. Harvey Publications All Rights Reserved.

The Romberg Sonata in C Major Study Book for Cello   3

Sonata, First Movement
Section One: Measures 1-16

Note: The Sonata is broken up into sections in this study book. The complete piece is at the back of the book.

Sonata Op. 43 No. 2, by Bernhard Romberg
edited by F. Jansen, C. Harvey
Exercises by Cassia Harvey

Learning the Notes and Listening for Intonation
Measures 1-3

©2018 C. Harvey Publications All Rights Reserved.

Learning the Notes and String Crossing
Measures 4, 8

Shifting to Third Position
Measures 5-6

The Romberg Sonata in C Major Study Book for Cello   5

Note: Sometimes it can help to draw a vertical line through a measure so that the eye can separate the notes more easily.

Shifting, Bowing, and Rhythm
Measure 5-7

staccato   *spiccato*

staccato   *spiccato*

Left and Right-Hand Agility
Measures 6-8

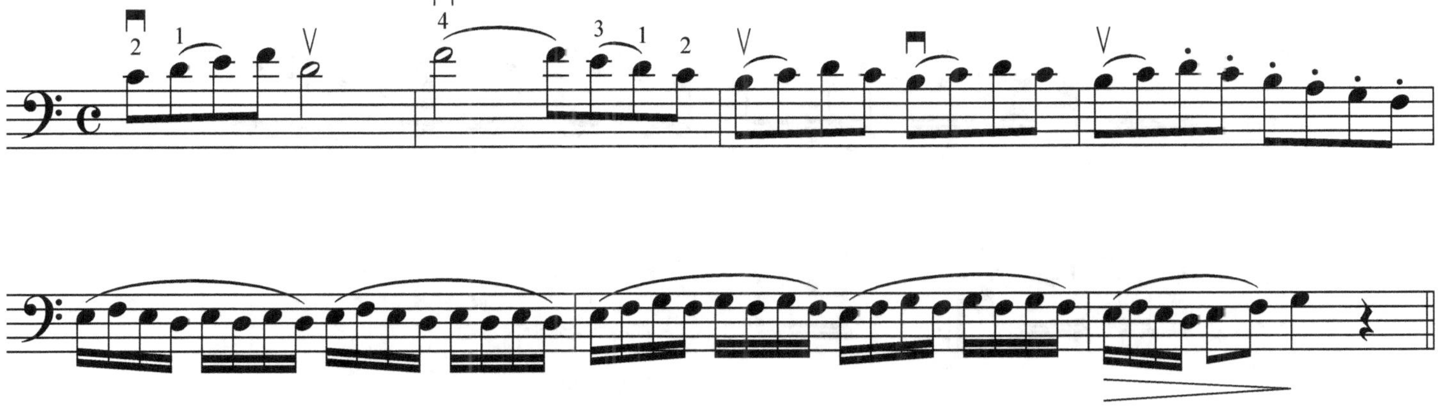

©2018 C. Harvey Publications All Rights Reserved.

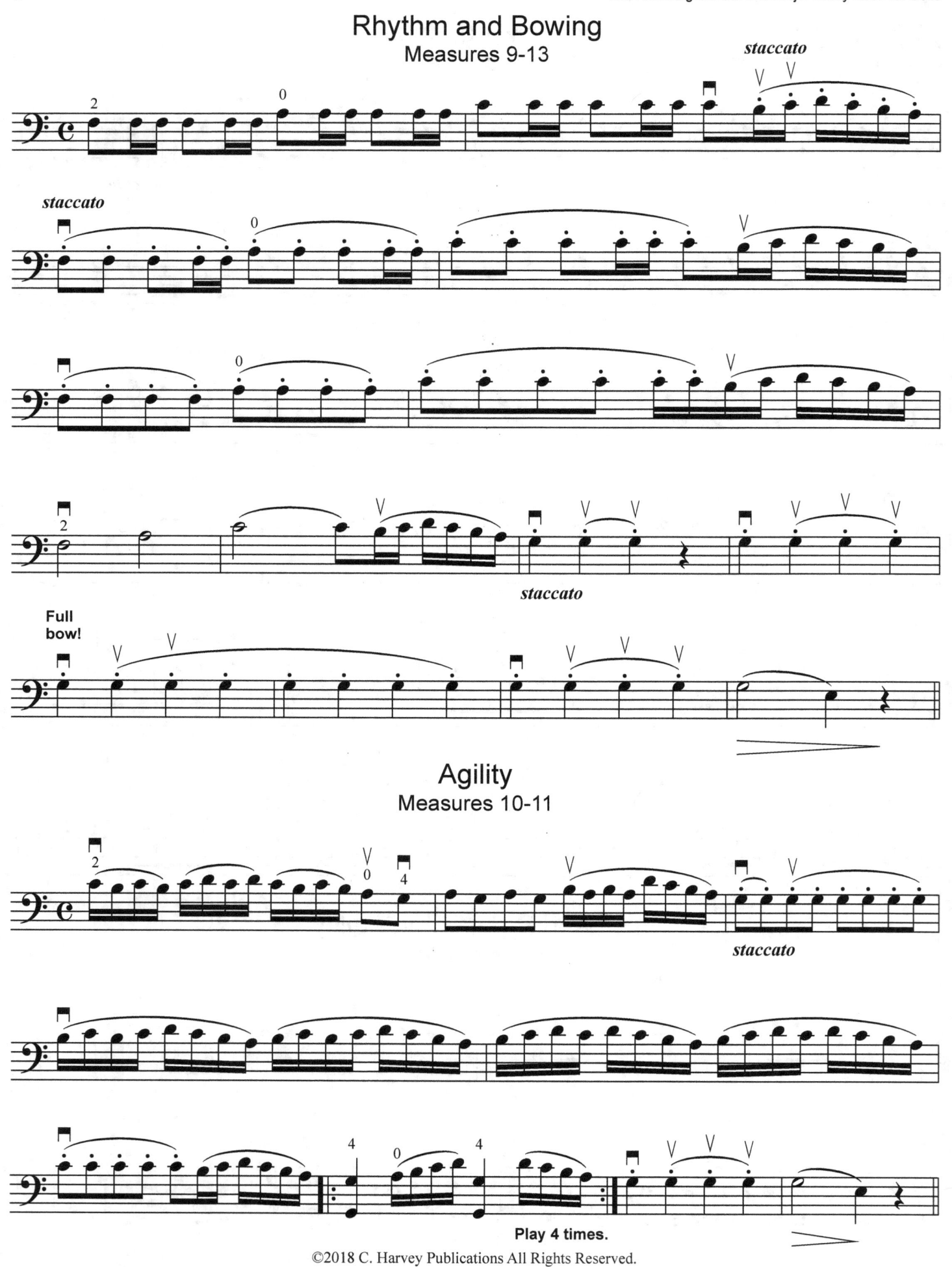

The Romberg Sonata in C Major Study Book for Cello

Shifting II: Measures 17-21

Shifting and Rhythm: Measures 17-22

©2018 C. Harvey Publications All Rights Reserved.

Shifting to Fourth Position
Measure 22

Shifting to A♭ and E♭
Measures 22-24

The Romberg Sonata in C Major Study Book for Cello 11

Start slowly to learn the notes.
Repeat the exercise several times
until you are playing as fast as possible.

©2018 C. Harvey Publications All Rights Reserved.

Learning the Notes II: Measures 29-40

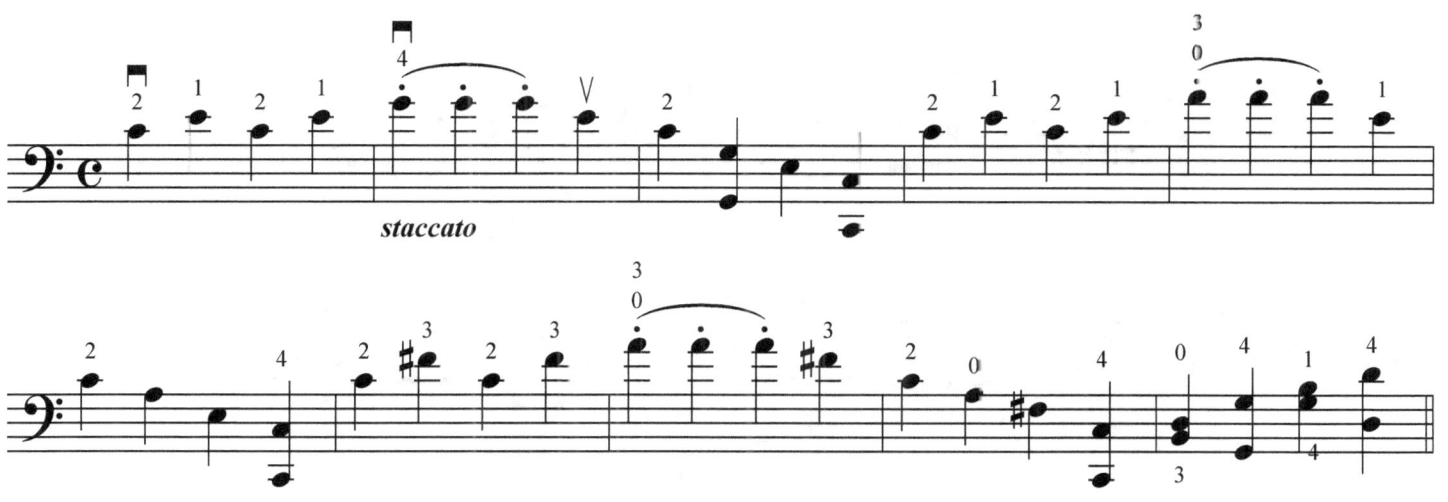

Rhythm and Bowing: Measure 41

Allow the bow to come off the string slightly on these up-bows.

Triplets into Eighth Notes: Measures 41-42

Note: Triplets are faster than regular eighth notes because 3 triplet notes have to fit into a beat instead of 2 eighth notes.

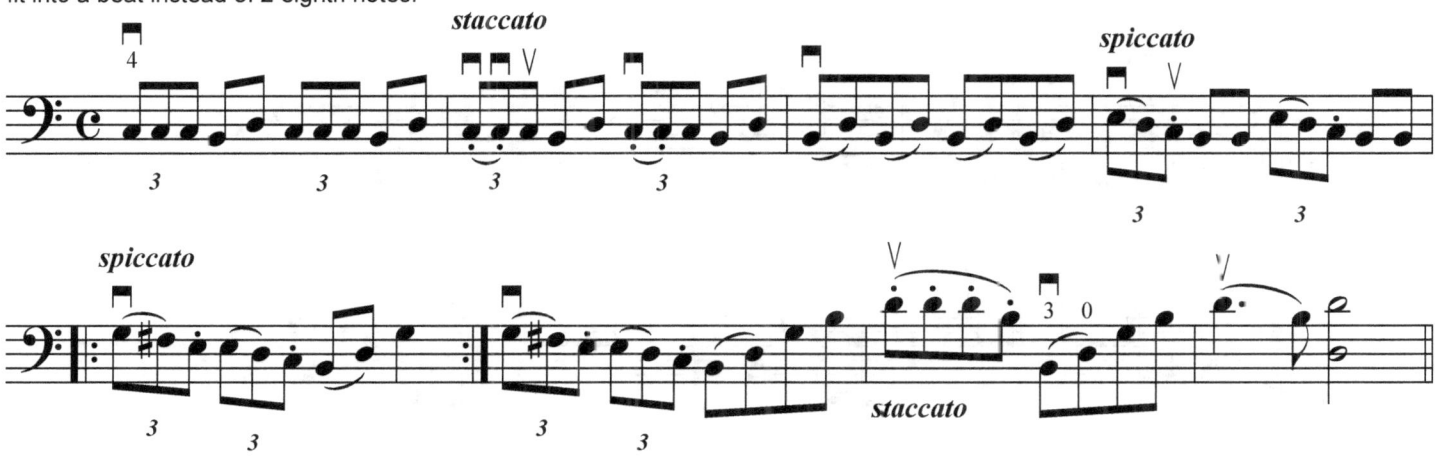

The Romberg Sonata in C Major Study Book for Cello

Learning the Notes and Bowing
Measure 43

Start slowly to learn the notes.
Repeat the exercise several times
until you are playing as fast as possible. ♩=100-140

Slowing Bow Speed in the Middle of the Run
Measure 44

♩=70-90

©2018 C. Harvey Publications All Rights Reserved.

Rhythm Overview
Measures 41-45

Sonata, First Movement
Section Four: Measures 49-69

Shifting, Trill, and Slow Up-Bow
Measures 49-51

Rhythm
Measures 52-58

Shifting
Measures 58-63

Rhythm, String Crossing, and Shifting
Measures 63-69

Sonata, First Movement
Section Five: Measures 70-80a

Intonation
Measures 70-71

Make sure the regular note sounds at the same pitch as the harmonic.

The Romberg Sonata in C Major Study Book for Cello — 21

Fifth Position I
Measures 71, 73

This is a pretty big space & might feel like an extension.

Reach back one whole step.

directly across

Reach across to the A string and up one whole step.

half step

half step

* For most of these exercises, it is better to play the high A as a regular (pressed down) note rather than as a harmonic, so that the exact distance and spacing can be learned.

Fifth Position II
Measures 71, 73-74

whole step

half step

(D string)

spiccato

©2018 C. Harvey Publications All Rights Reserved.

Fluency
Measures 70-73

Mapping the Notes on the D string: Measures 74-75

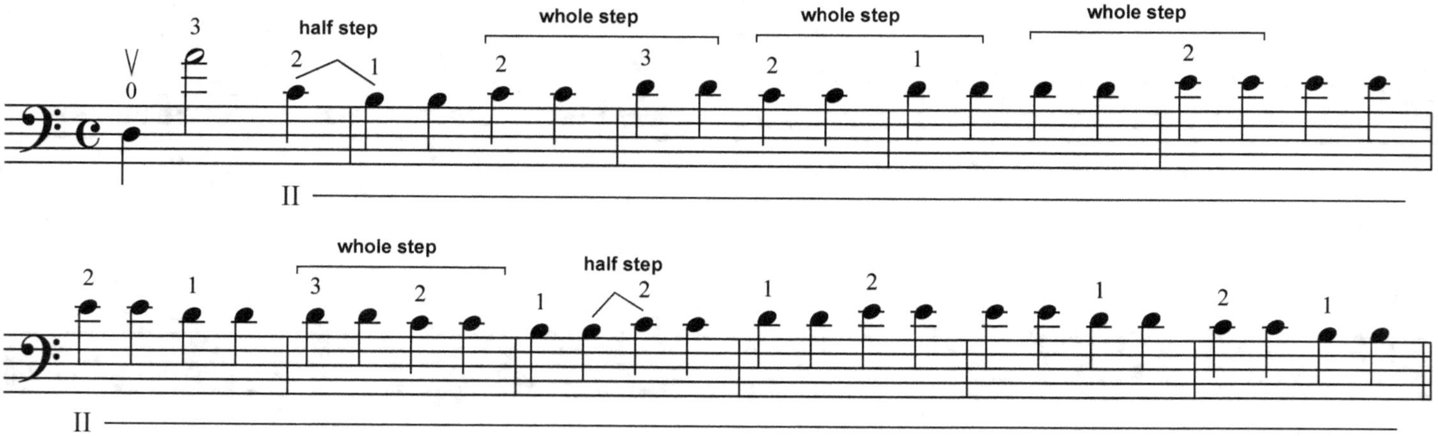

The Romberg Sonata in C Major Study Book for Cello   23

Learning the Notes I
Measures 74-76

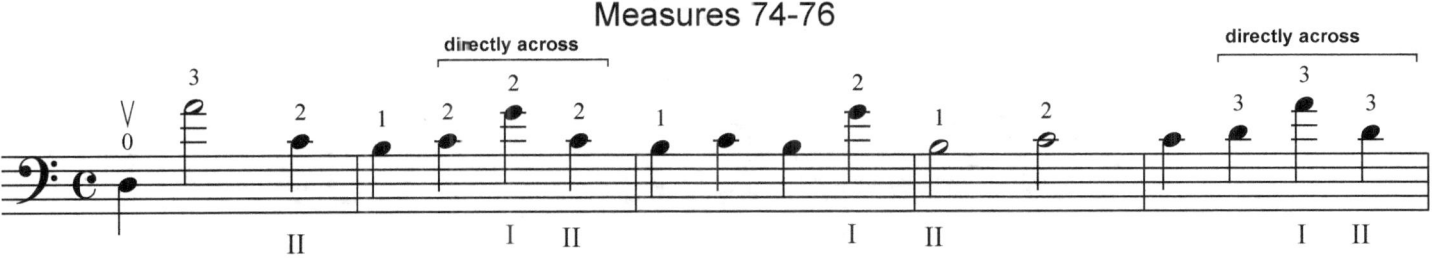

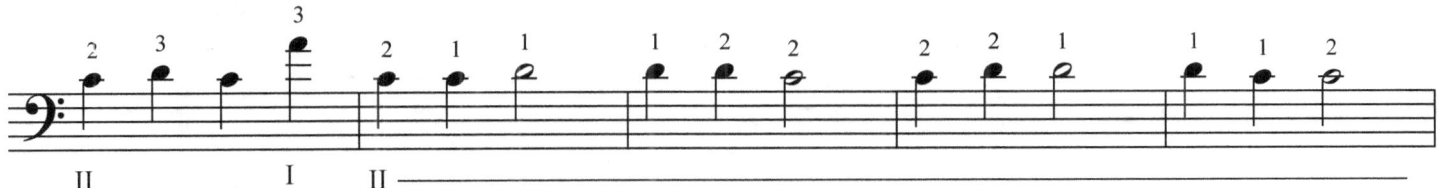

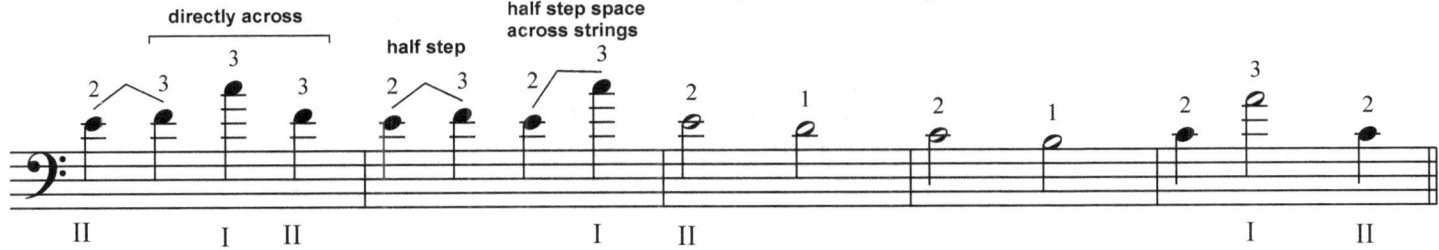

Learning the Notes II
Measures 74-76

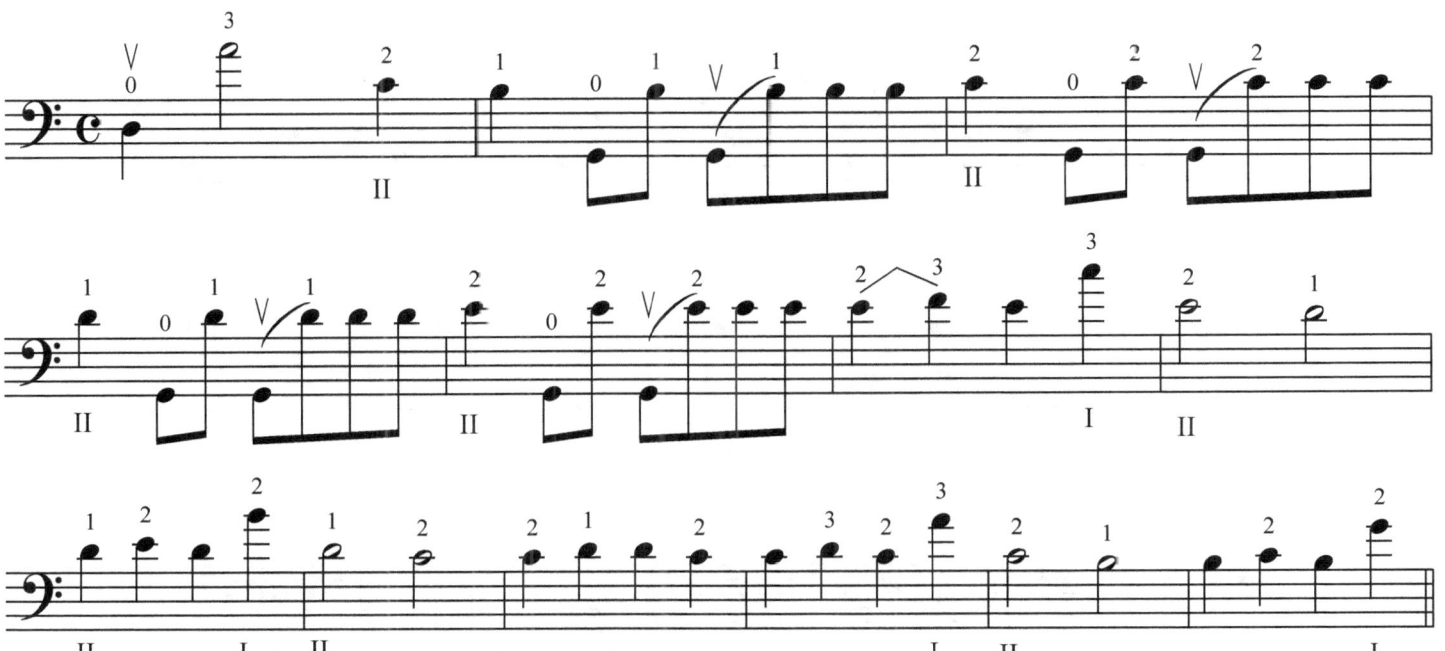

©2018 C. Harvey Publications All Rights Reserved.

Rhythm
Measures 73-76

Finger Exercise I
Measures 74-75

Finger Exercise II
Measure 75

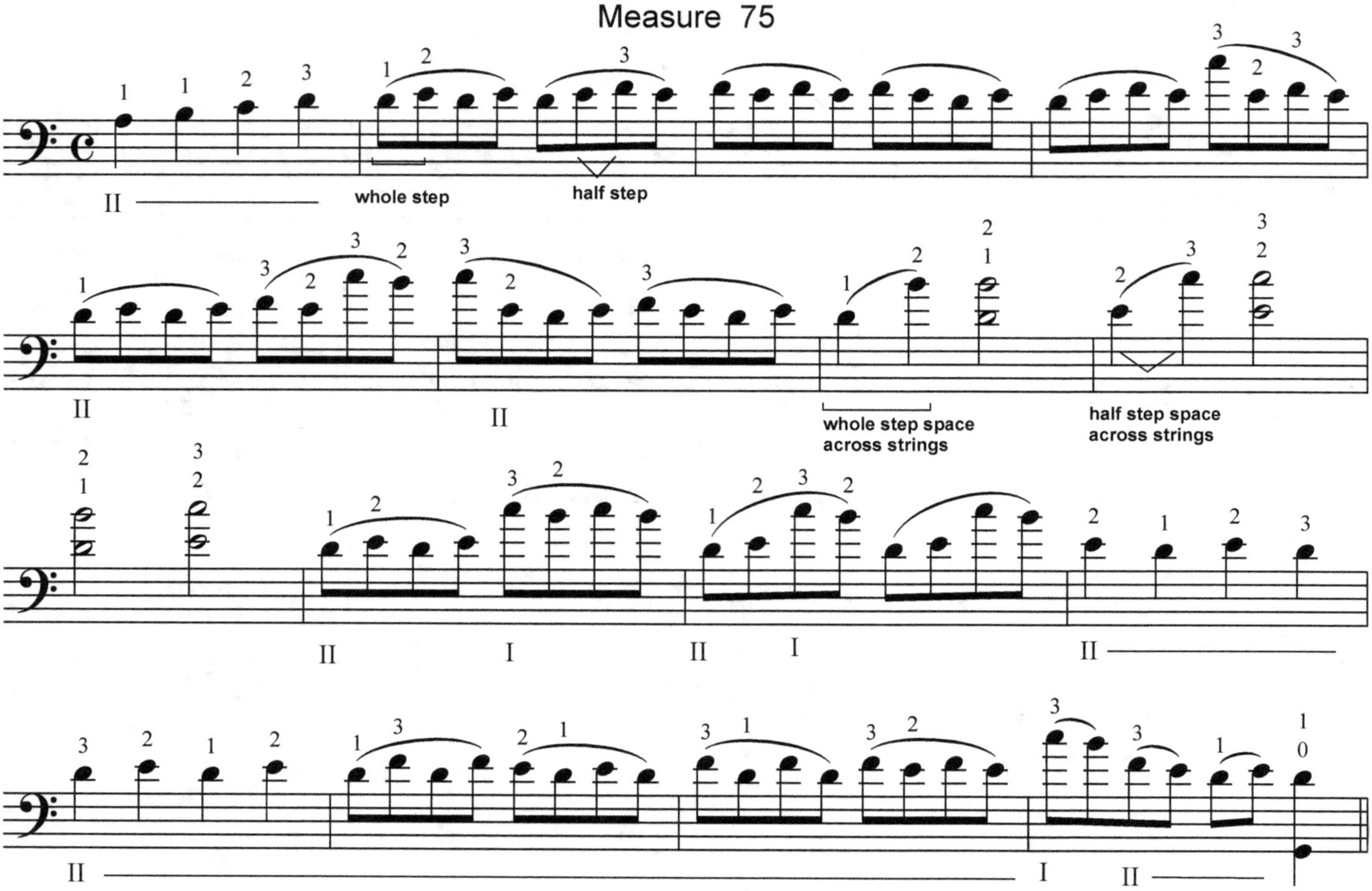

Optional: Advanced Double Stops for Intonation & Spacing
Measures 74-75

©2018 C. Harvey Publications All Rights Reserved.

The Romberg Sonata in C Major Study Book for Cello

Fluency I: Measures 73-75

Start on an up-bow here!

Fluency II: Measures 73-75

Start on an up-bow here!

spiccato

©2018 C. Harvey Publications All Rights Reserved.

Agility
Measures 76-79

Note: The dots that are "missing" in some of these measures reflect the dots that are not included in the early Romberg editions.

Sonata, First Movement
Section Six: Measures 80-91

Slowing the Bow Down
Measures 79-80

The Romberg Sonata in C Major Study Book for Cello 31

Shifting II
Measure 84

Shifting III
Measures 84-86

©2018 C. Harvey Publications All Rights Reserved.

Agility and Bowing: Measure 87

Shifting: Measure 89

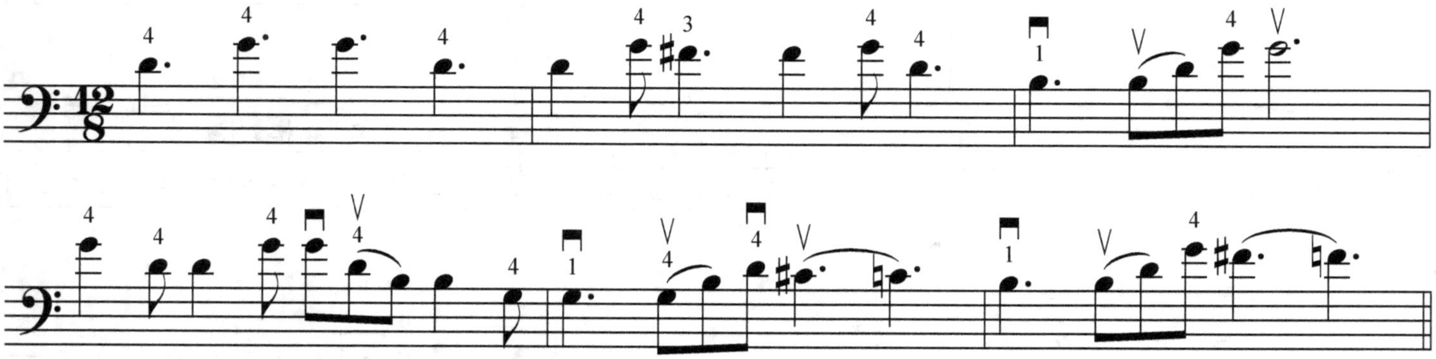

Staccato for Bow Agility: Measures 86-89

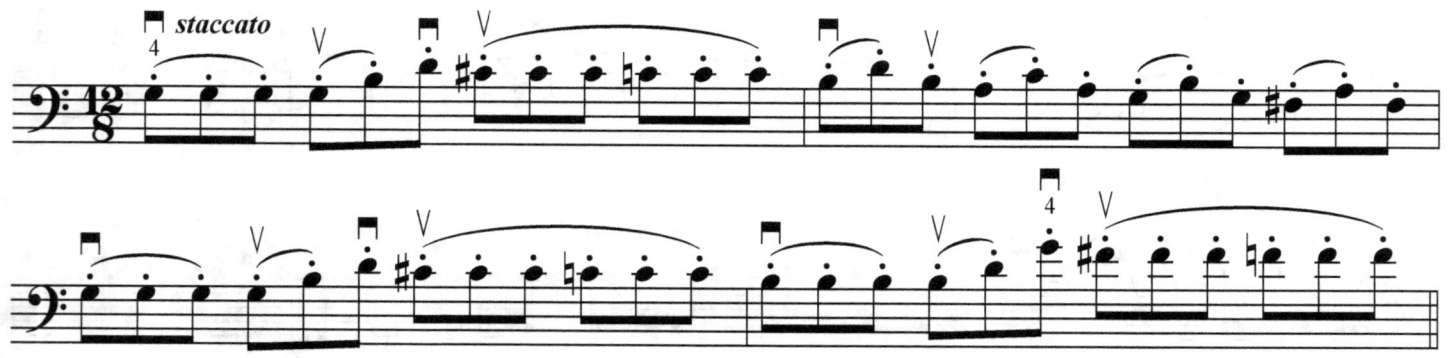

Shifting: Measures 90-91

Sonata, First Movement
Section Seven: Measures 92-112

Intonation
Measures 92-100

Finger and Bow Agility
Measures 95, 101

The Romberg Sonata in C Major Study Book for Cello 35

Finding Fifth Position
Measure 104

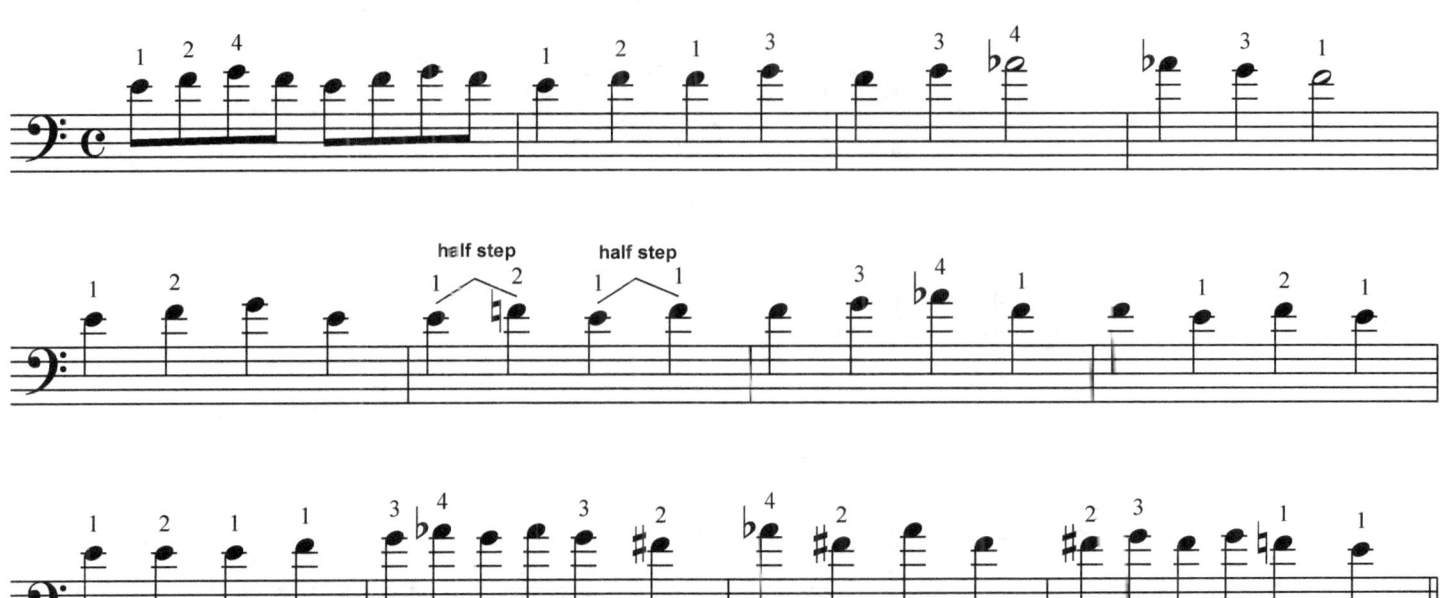

Rhythm and Shifting
Measures 99-104

Note: The + sign indicates left-hand pizzicato. Pick the bow up off of the string and, using any finger of the left-hand, pluck the string. In this exercise, the pizzicato is used to help you feel the rhythm of the rest.

staccato

©2015 C. Harvey Publications All Rights Reserved.

Shifting I
Measures 103-104

Shifting II
Measures 103-106

The Romberg Sonata in C Major Study Book for Cello

Learning the Notes
Measure 107-112

Sonata, First Movement
Section Eight: Measures 113-128

Bowing I
Measures 113, 115

Left and Right-Hand Agility
Measures 113-116

Fluency
Measures 113-116

Repeat this exercise as many times as you wish, playing faster each time.

spiccato

The Romberg Sonata in C Major Study Book for Cello

Shifting
Measures 121-128

Double Stops for Hand Strength
Measures 117-126

Bow Control
Measures 117-122

Quick Shifting
Measures 121-128

Repeat this exercise as many times as you wish, playing faster each time.

Fluency
Measures 122-128

Sonata, First Movement
Section Nine: Measures 129-141a

Flatten first finger across two strings for the double stop fifths in this exercise.

"Barring" the First Finger Across Strings
Measures 129-130, 133-134

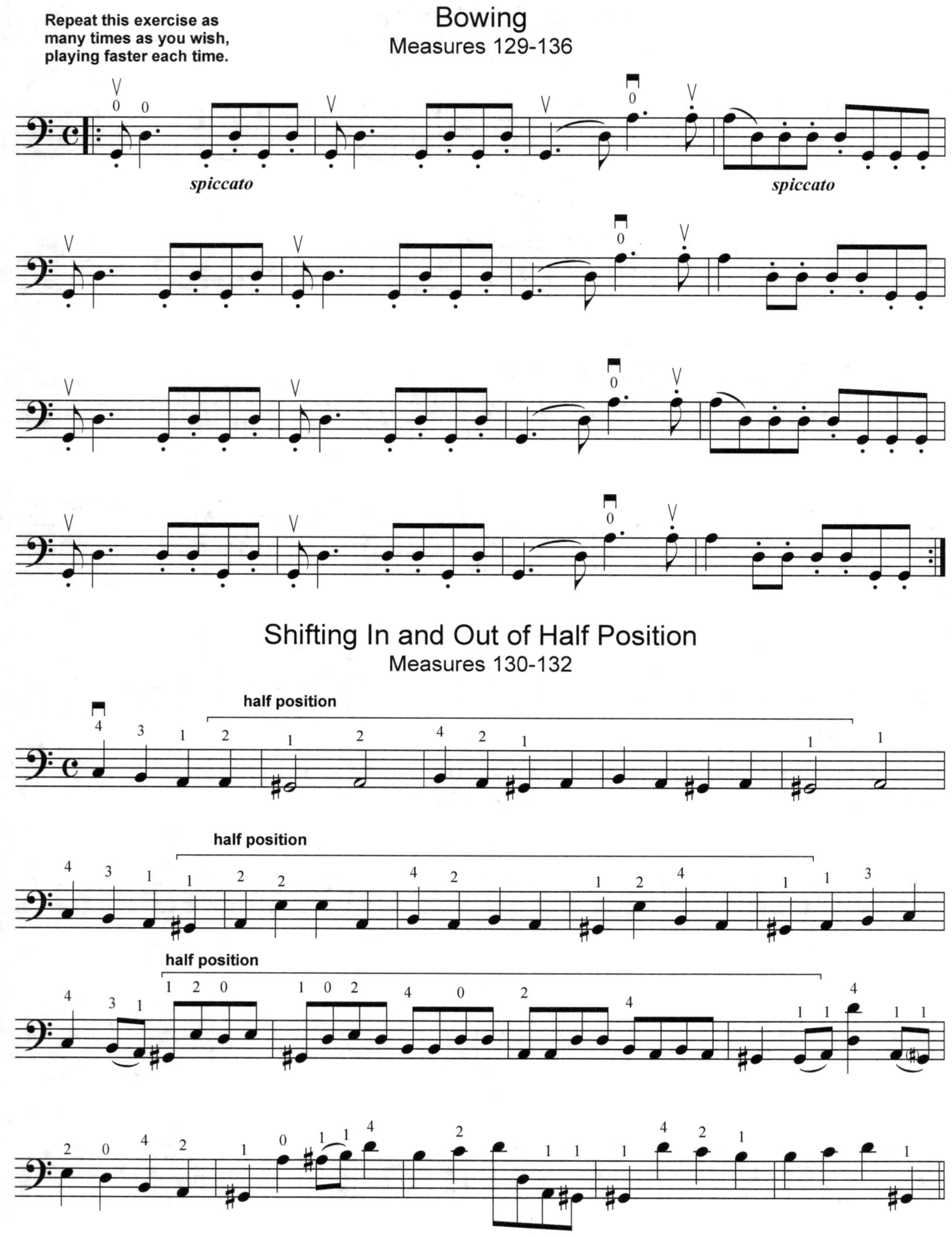

Double Stops for Agility
Measures 129-137

Bowing and Bow Speed
Measures 135-138

Intonation
Measures 131-132

Finger Exercise
Measures 130, 132, 136

Repeat the exercise several times until you are playing as fast as possible.

The Romberg Sonata in C Major Study Book for Cello

Fluency: Measures 129-136

* Note: It is not necessary to play the dotted eighth notes off the string, however they should be light (leggiero).

Shifting I: Measures 137-141a

©2008 C. Harvey Publications All Rights Reserved.

Shifting II
Measures 137-141a

Sonata, First Movement
Section Ten: Measures 141-158

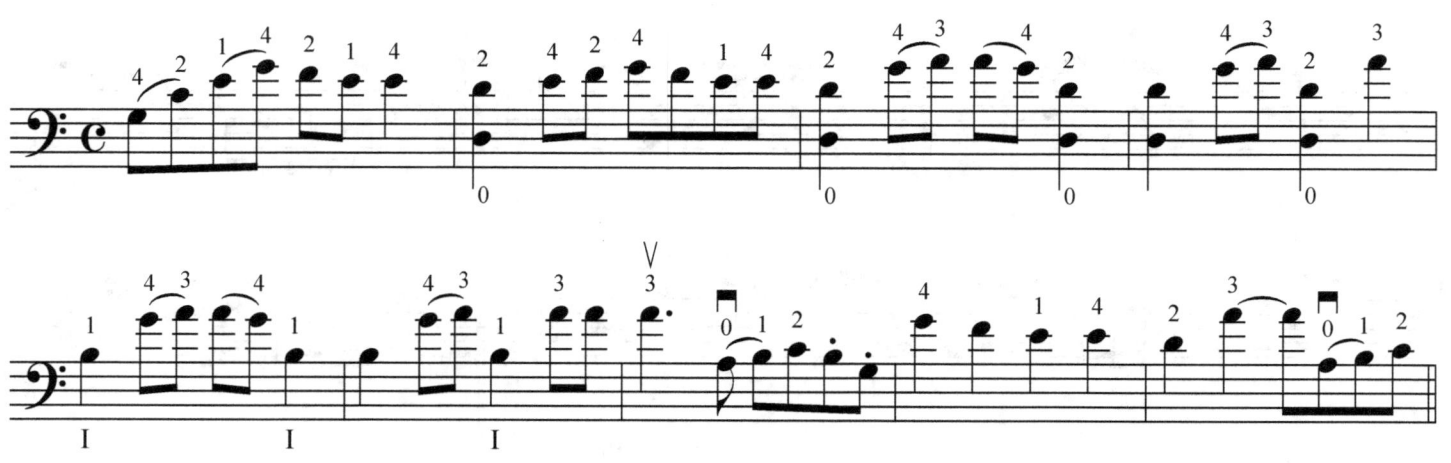

The Romberg Sonata in C Major Study Book for Cello

Shifting
Measures 141-143

Rhythm and Extensions
Measures 142-144

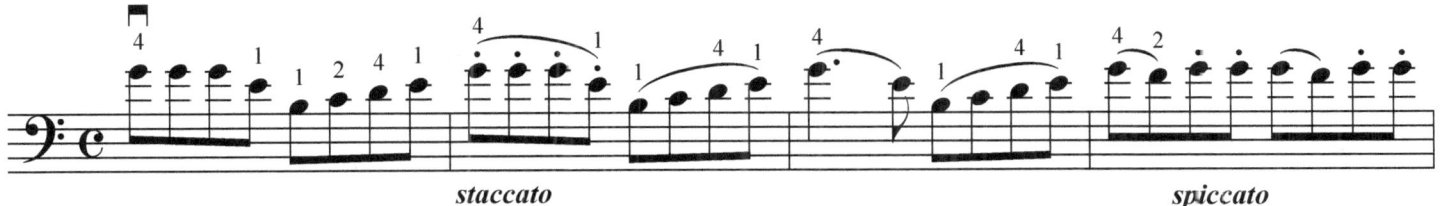

Double Stops for Intonation
Measures 143-145

©2018 C. Harvey Publications All Rights Reserved.

Reaching 4th Finger Sharps
Measures 144-146

String Crossing
Measures 145-146

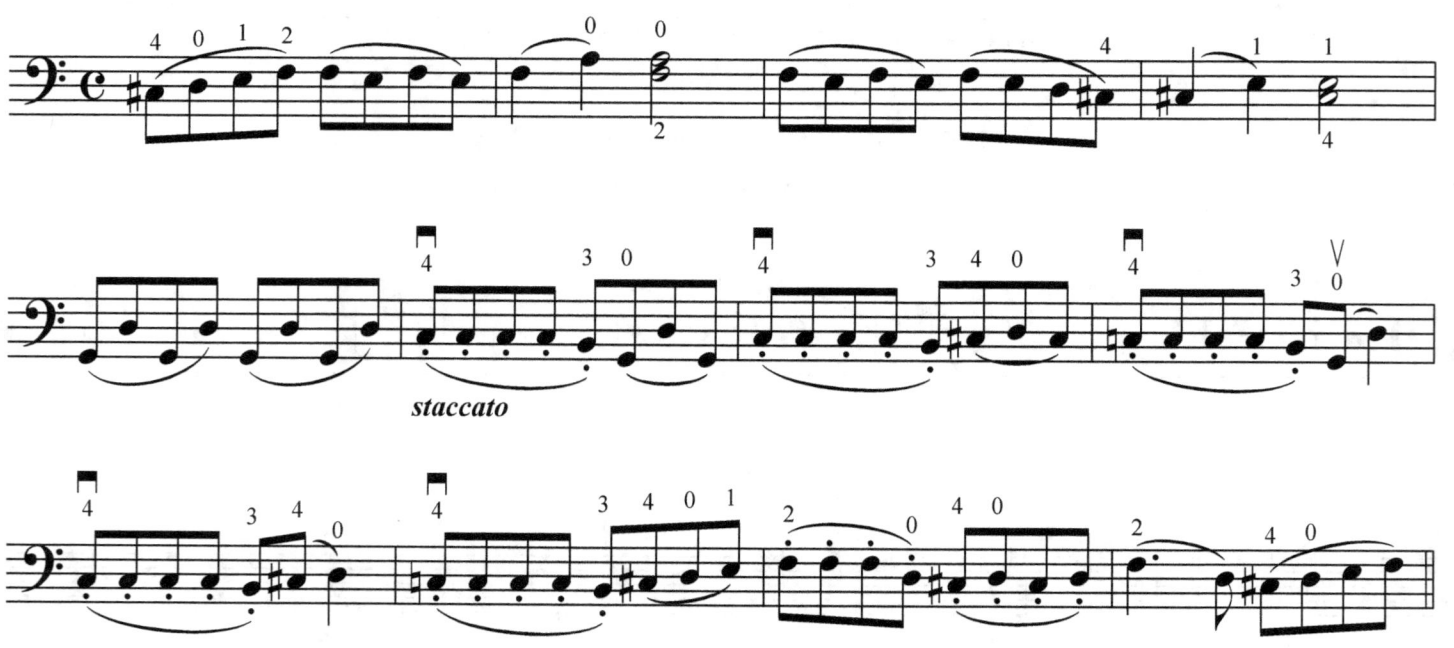

©2018 C. Harvey Publications All Rights Reserved.

The Romberg Sonata in C Major Study Book for Cello 51

Finger Exercise
Measures 145-146

Shifting I
Measures 147-150

Shifting II
Measures 147-150

©2018 C. Harvey Publications All Rights Reserved.

Bowing
Measures 150-152

Repeat this exercise as many times as you wish, playing faster each time.

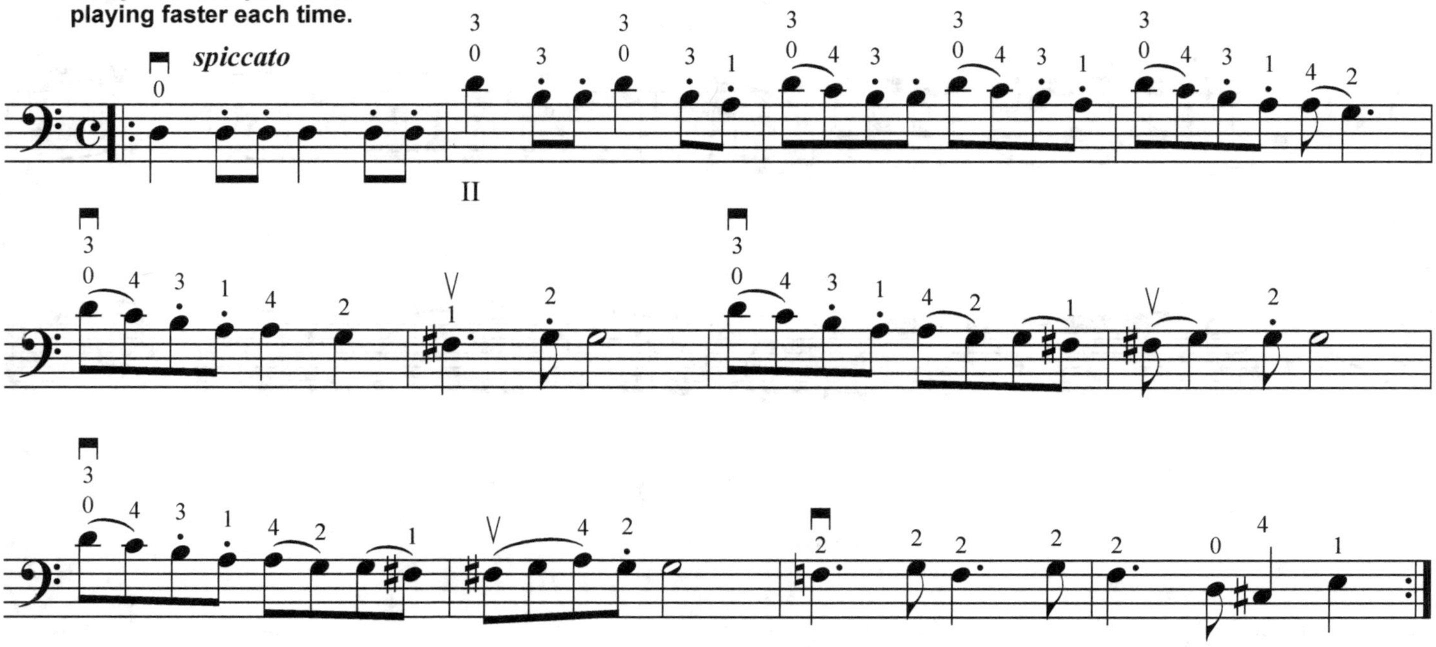

Bow Agility
Measures 152-156

Bowing and Shifting
Measures 157-158

Fluency
Measures 154-158

Sonata, First Movement
Section Eleven: Measures 159-166

Bowing on Open Strings: Measures 159-164

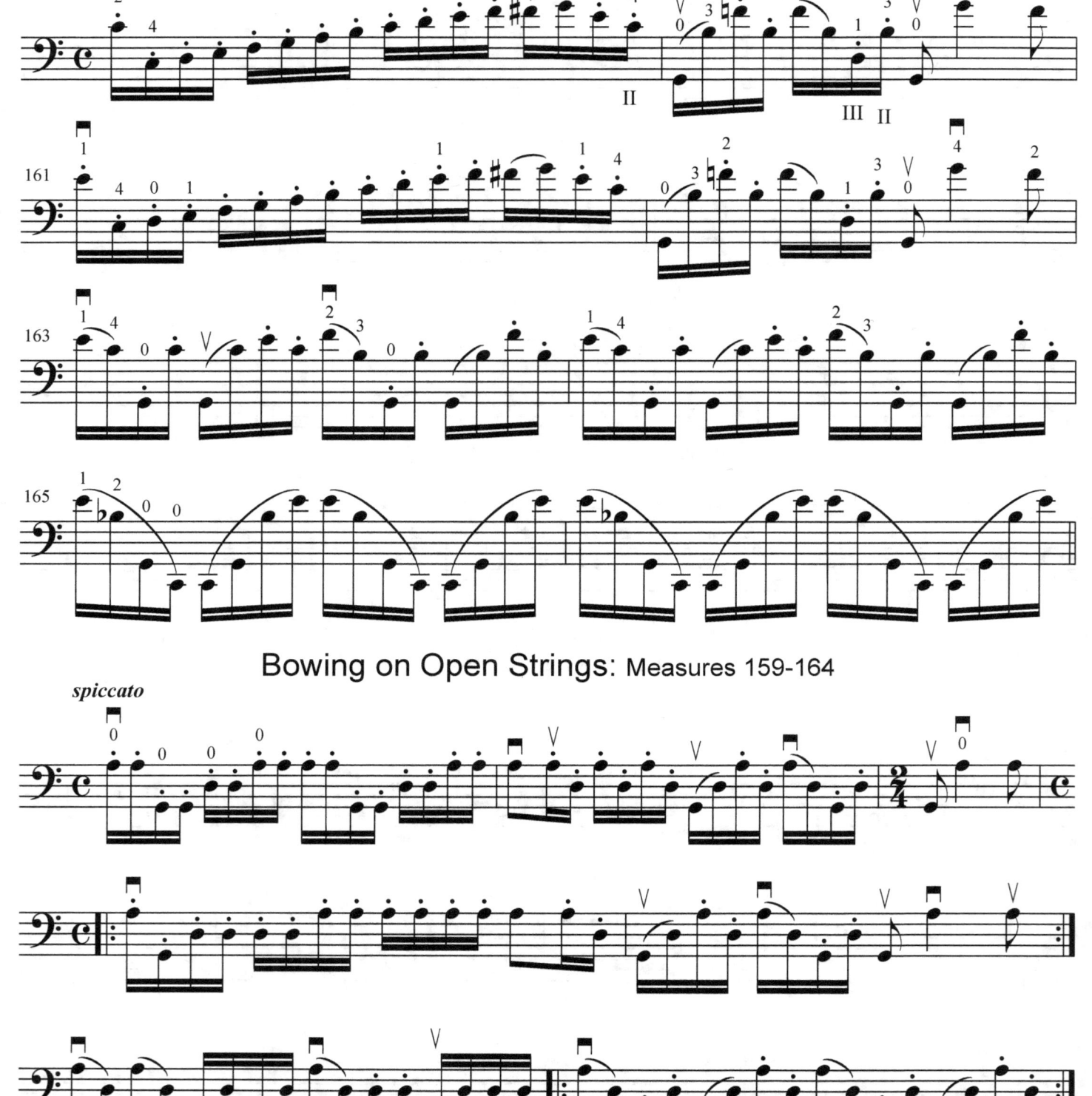

Bowing Study: Measures 159, 161

String Crossing I: Measures 160-162

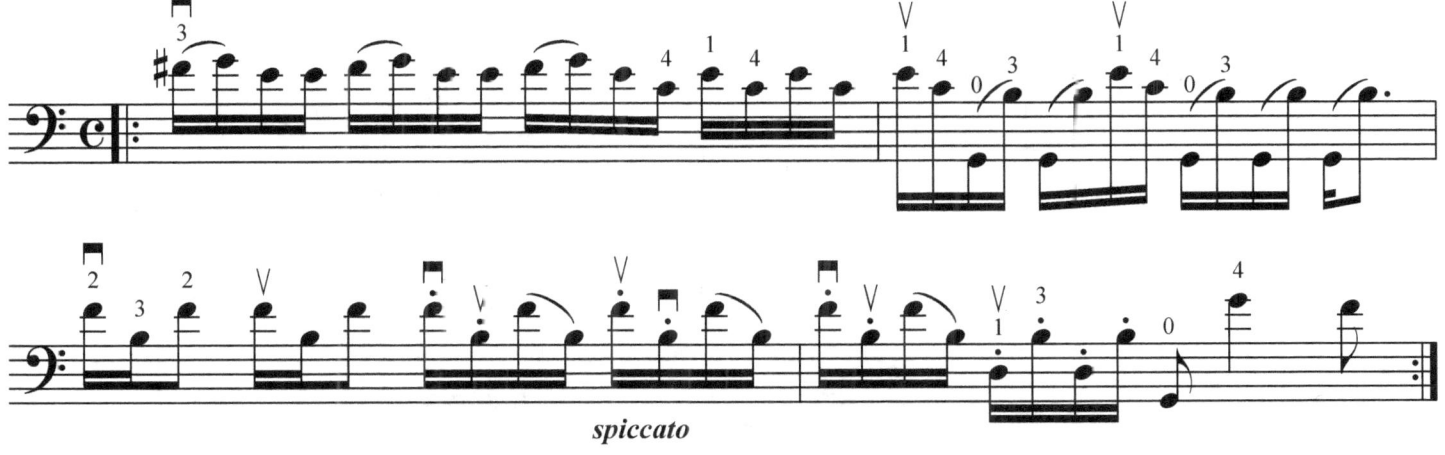

String Crossing II: Measures 160-162

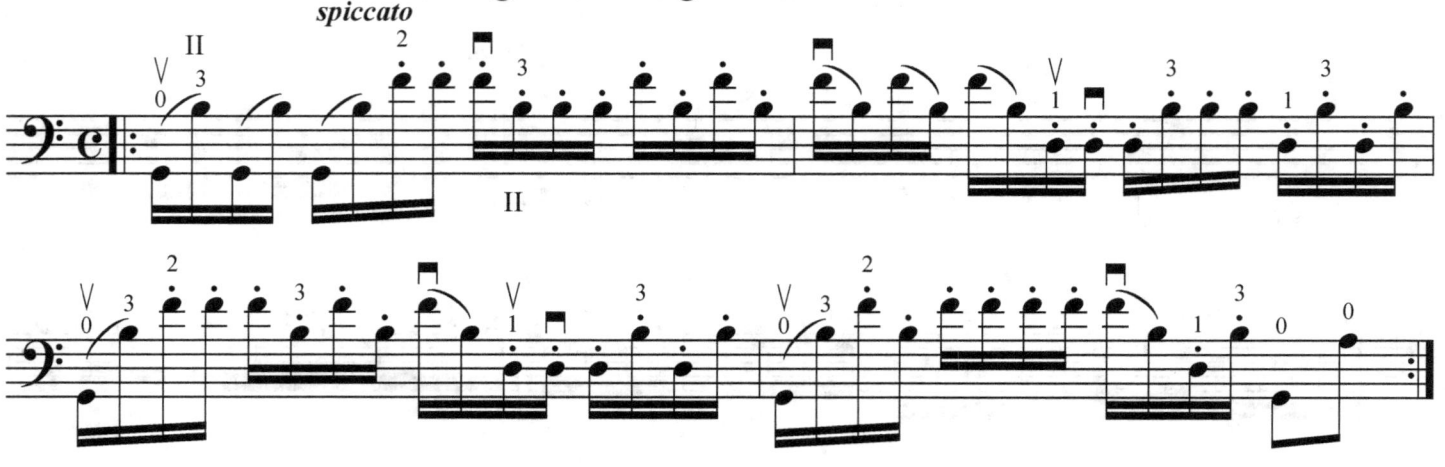

String Crossing III: Measures 160-162

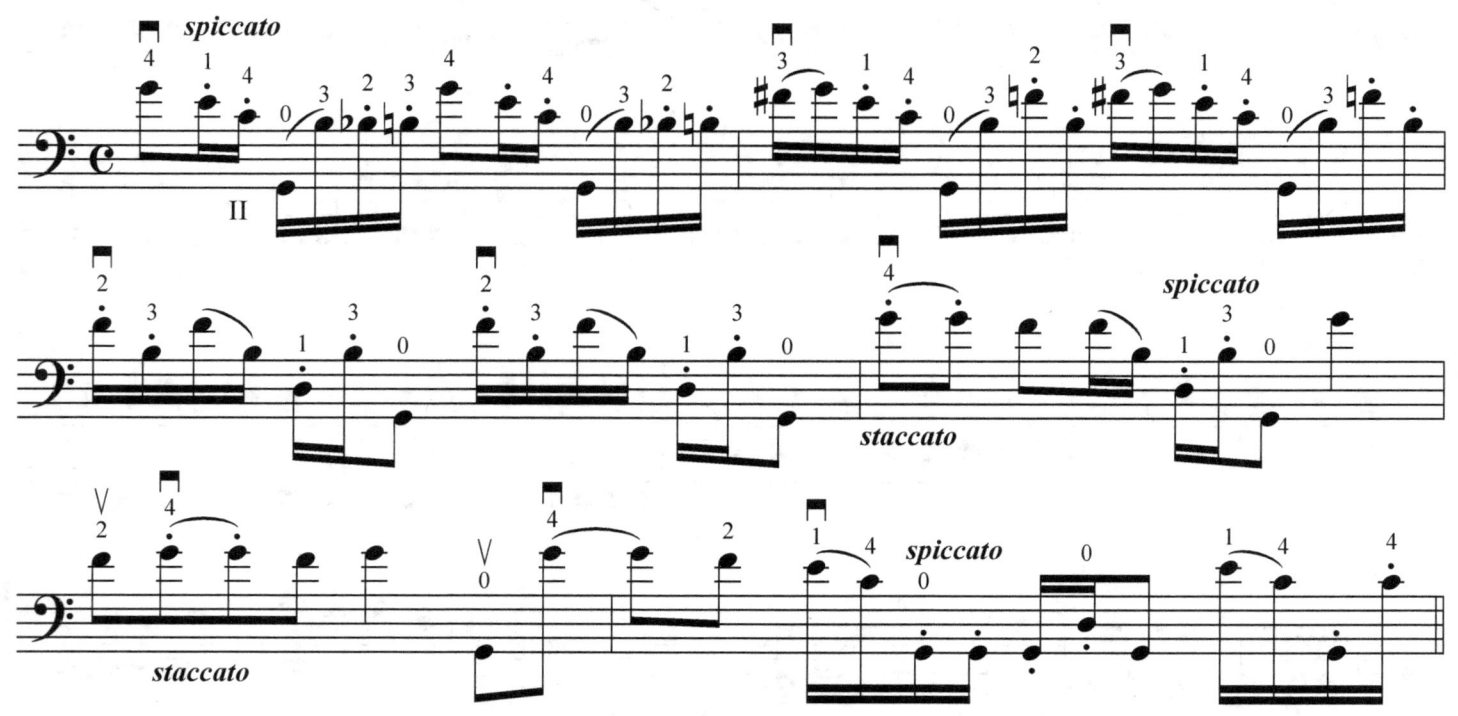

String Crossing and Spiccato: Measures 159-162

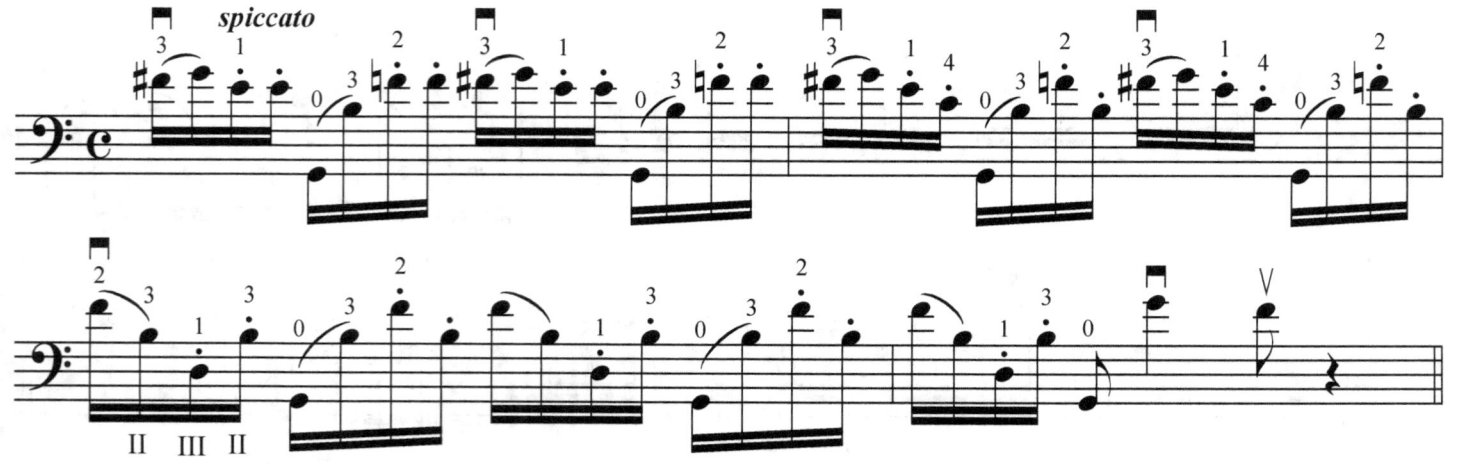

©2018 C. Harvey Publications All Rights Reserved.

The Romberg Sonata in C Major Study Book for Cello 57

Across Strings in Fourth Position: Measures 163-166

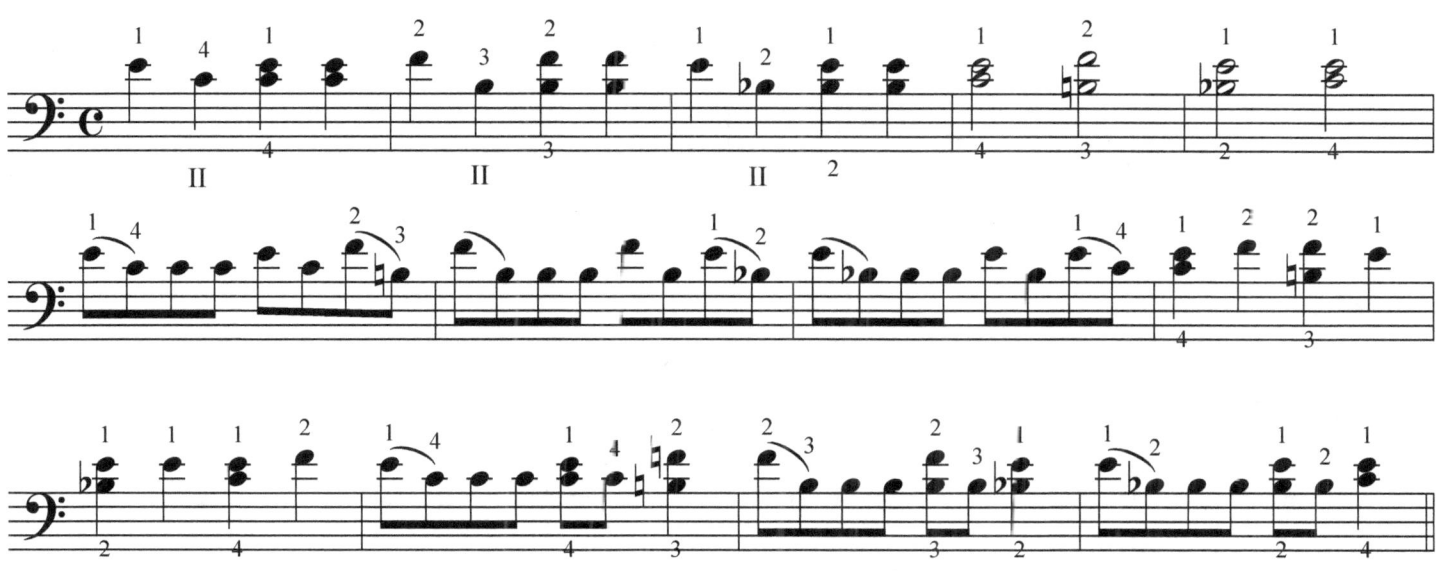

String Crossing I: Measures 163-164

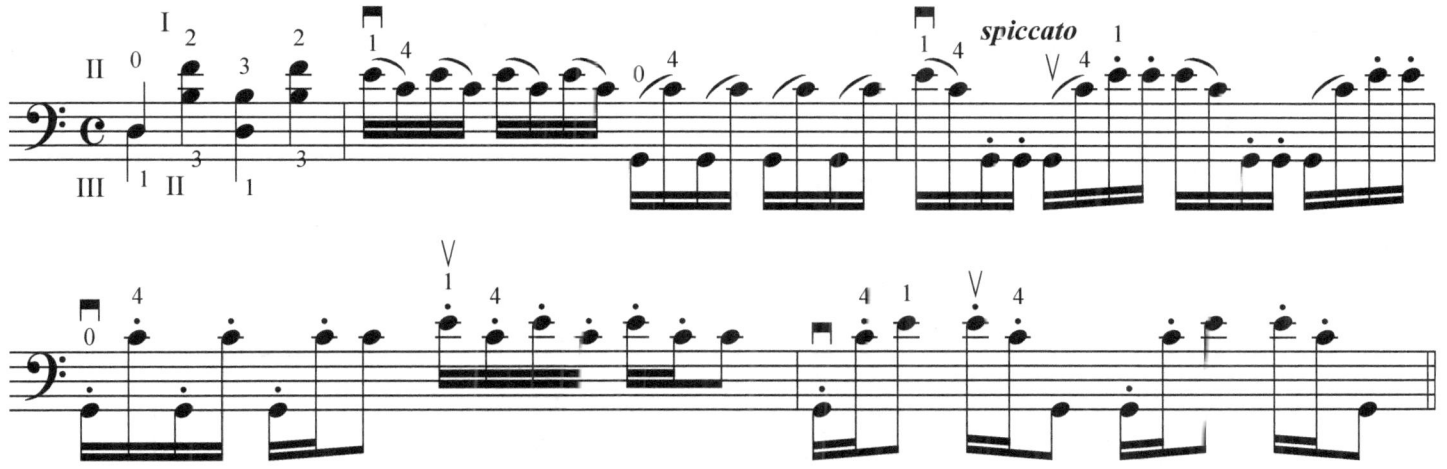

String Crossing II: Measures 163-164

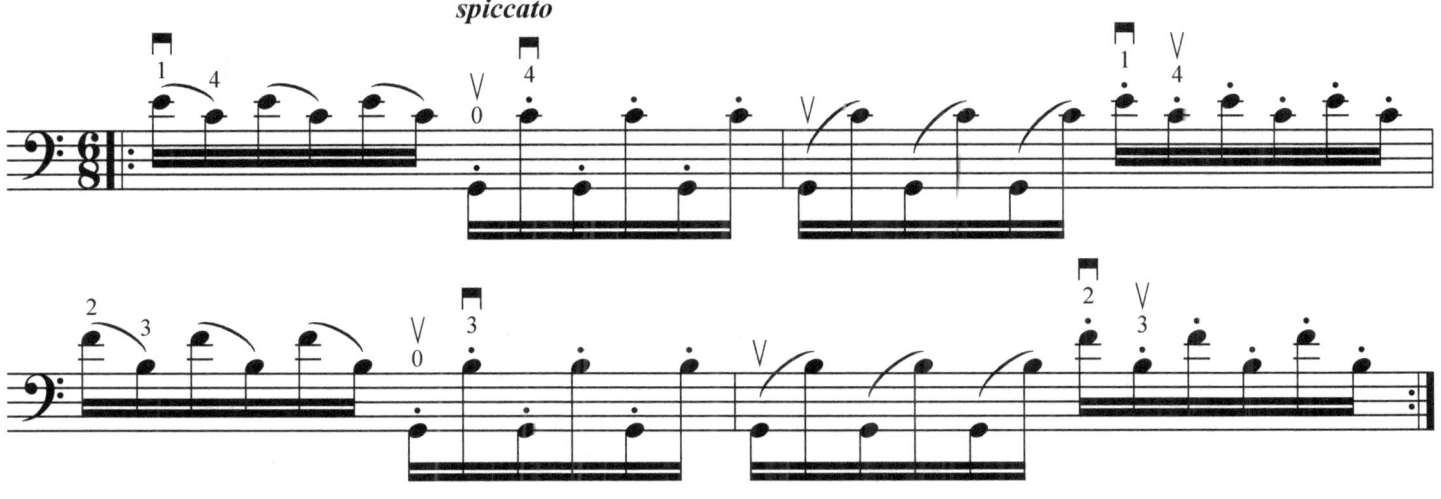

©2018 C. Harvey Publications All Rights Reserved.

String Crossing III: Measures 163-164

String Crossing: Measures 165-166

Sonata, First Movement
Section Twelve: Measures 167-186 (end of movement)

Shifting I: Measure 167

Shifting II
Measure 167

Double Stops for Intonation
Measures 168-171

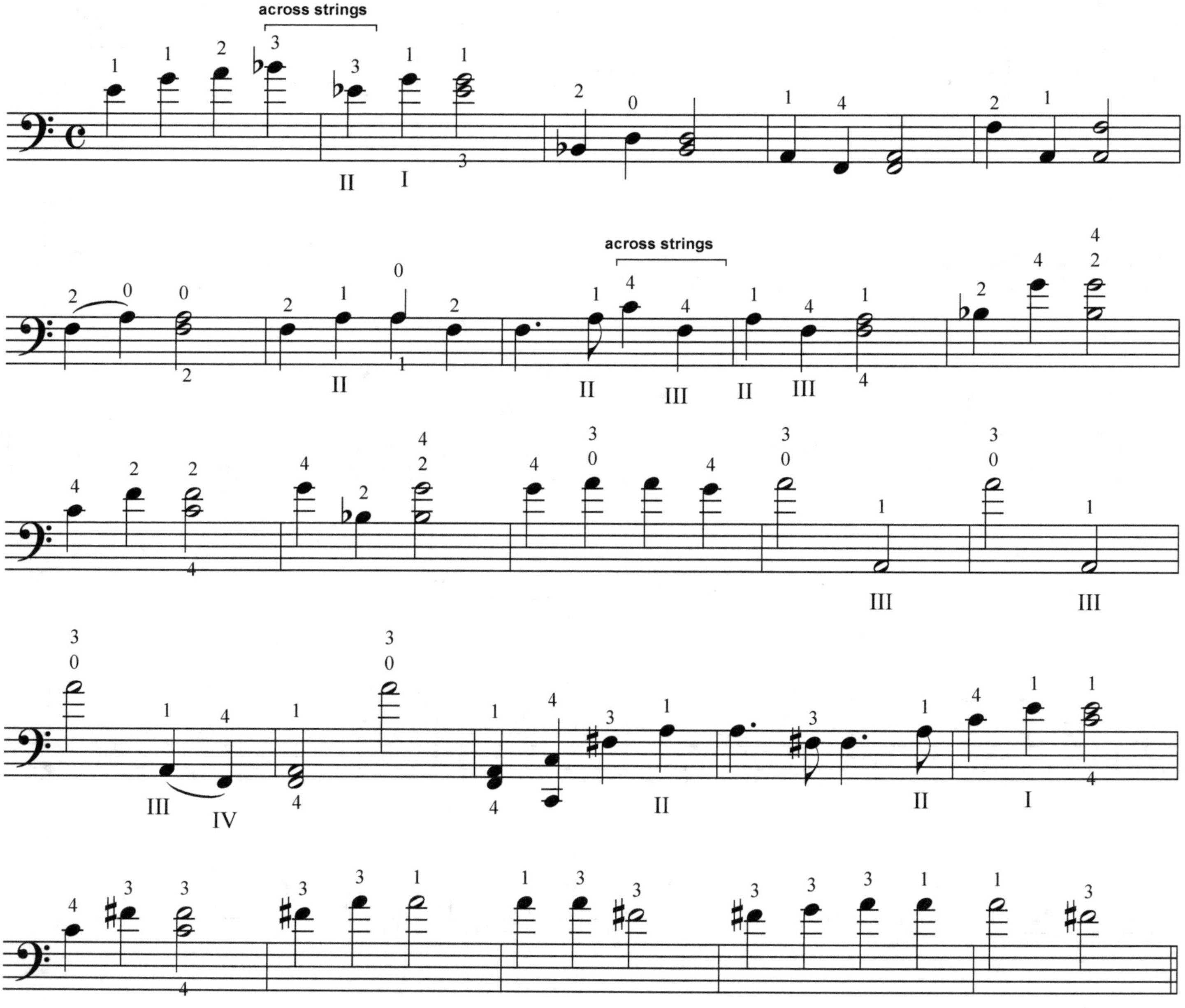

The Romberg Sonata in C Major Study Book for Cello

Shifting: Measures 170-171

Bowing: Measure 167-171

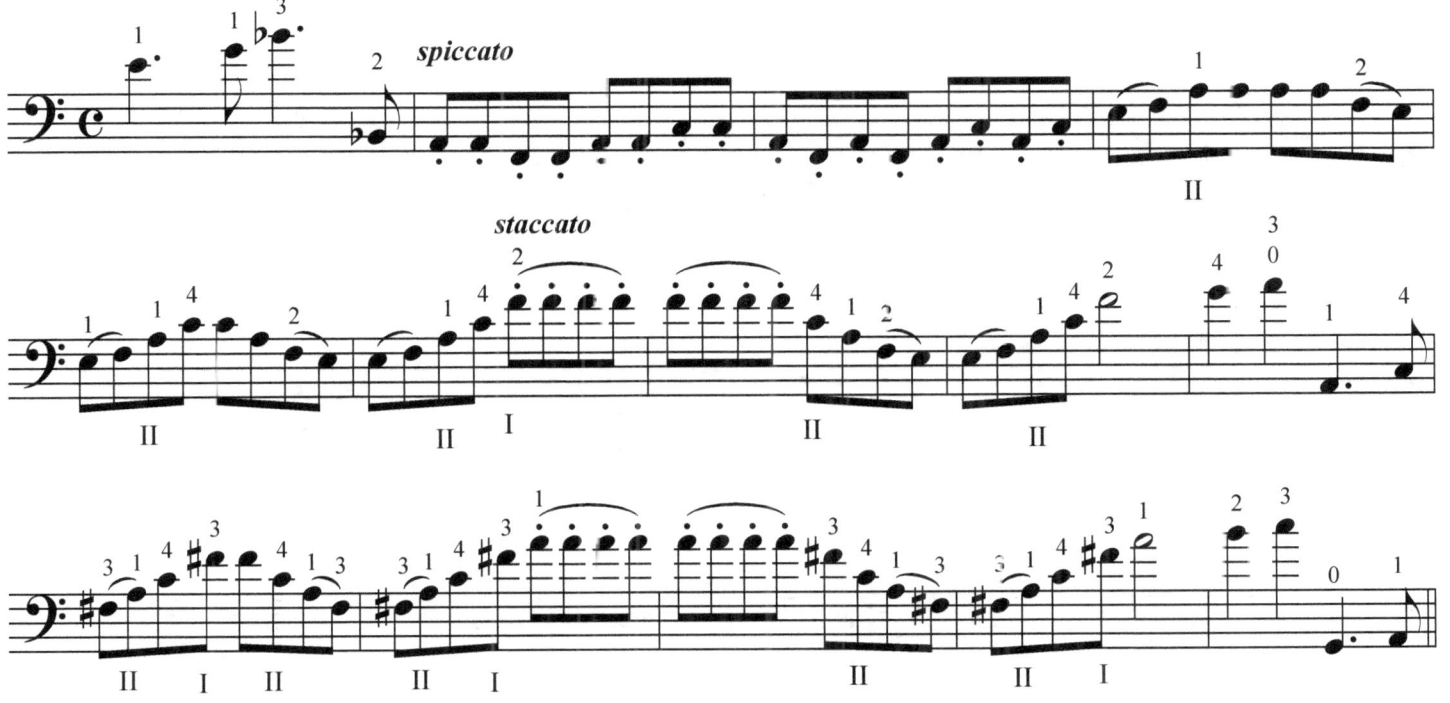

©2018 C. Harvey Publications All Rights Reserved.

Little Scale and Trill
Measure 172-175

Rhythm and Bowing
Measures 175-176

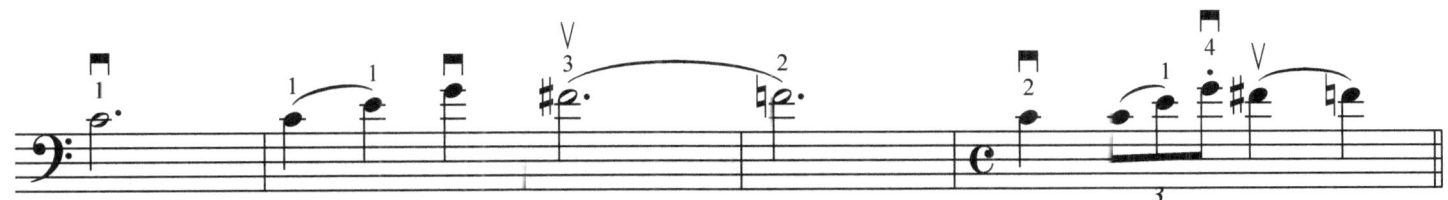

Bowing and Shifting
Measures 175-178

Changing Spacing in Sixth Position
Measure 178

Note: Only the half steps are marked here. If the step is not marked, you can assume it is a whole step.

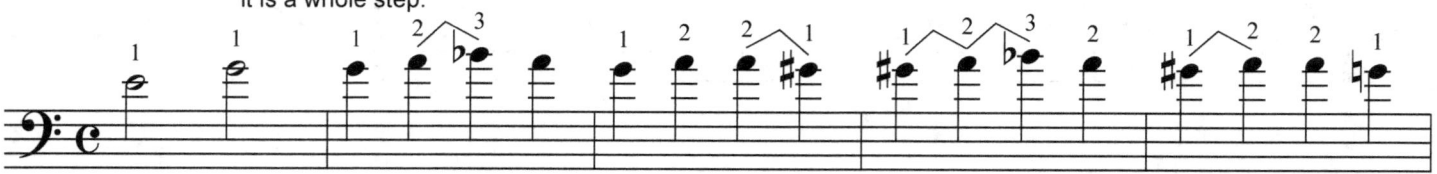

Rhythmic Shifting I
Measures 177-179

Rhythmic Shifting II
Measures 177-182

Rhythmic Shifting III
Measures 177-183

Shifting in Double Stops: Measures 183-186

Shifting Etude: Measures 167-186

Sonata, Second Movement
Section One: Measures 1-12

♪ = 1 beat ♩ = 2 beats ♩. = 3 beats

Note: Dots over notes in this movement are played as graceful staccato. The bow may come up off the string a little bit to keep the sound light.

Andante

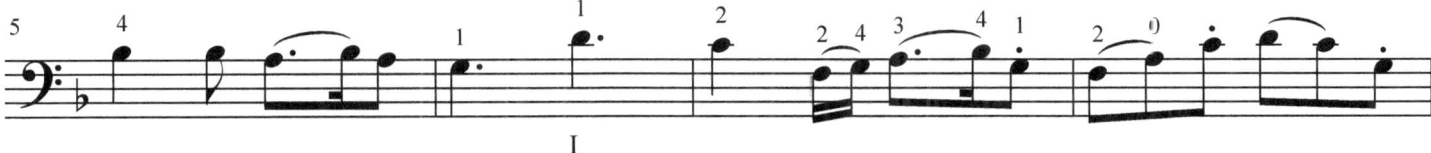

Shifting and String Crossing
Measures 1-7

©2018 C. Harvey Publications All Rights Reserved.

Shifting
Measures 1-12

Rhythmic Shifting
Measures 7-12

Rhythm and Bowing
Measures 1-12

Sonata, Second Movement
Section Two: Measures 13-27

Learning the Notes
Measures 13-15

Learning the Notes in Each Position
Measures 24-25

Shifting and String Crossing
Measures 24-25

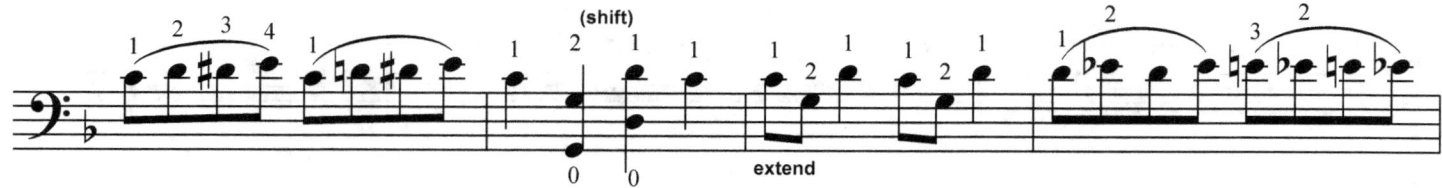

Fluency
Measures 24-27

Sonata, Second Movement
Section Three: Measures 28-36

Shifting
Measures 28-31

Regulating Bow Speed
Measures 28-31

Shifting
Measures 31-33

First Finger Placement: Measure 36

String Crossing I: Measures 33-36

String Crossing II: Measures 33-36

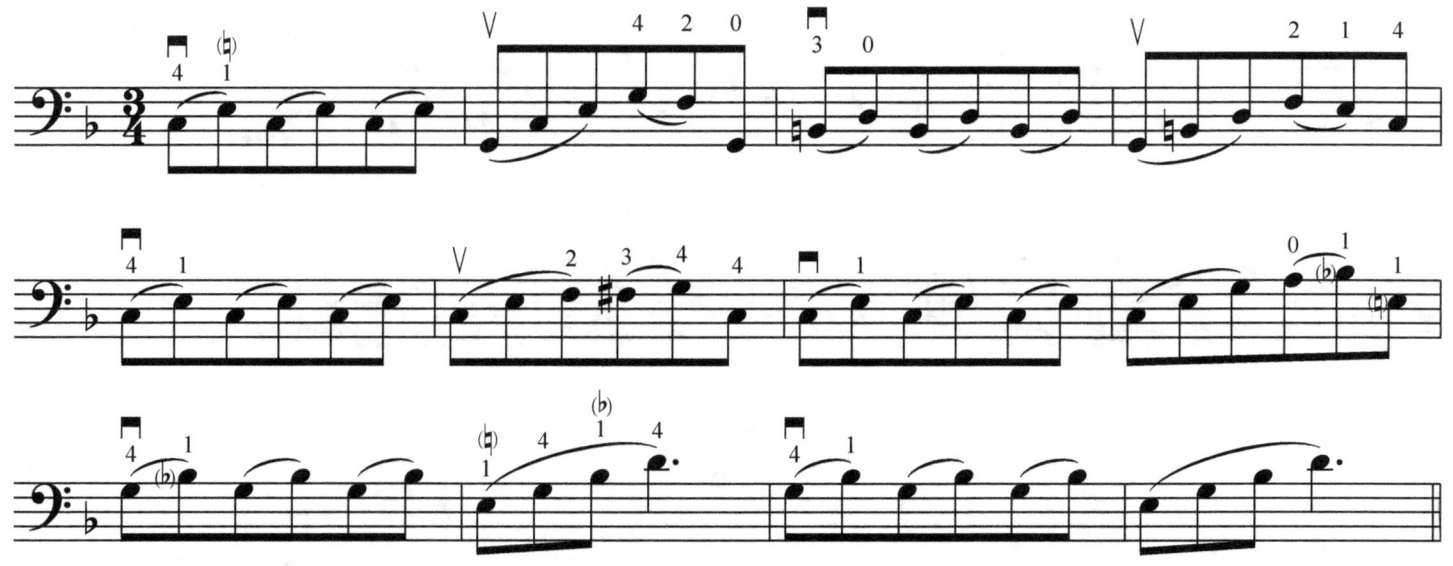

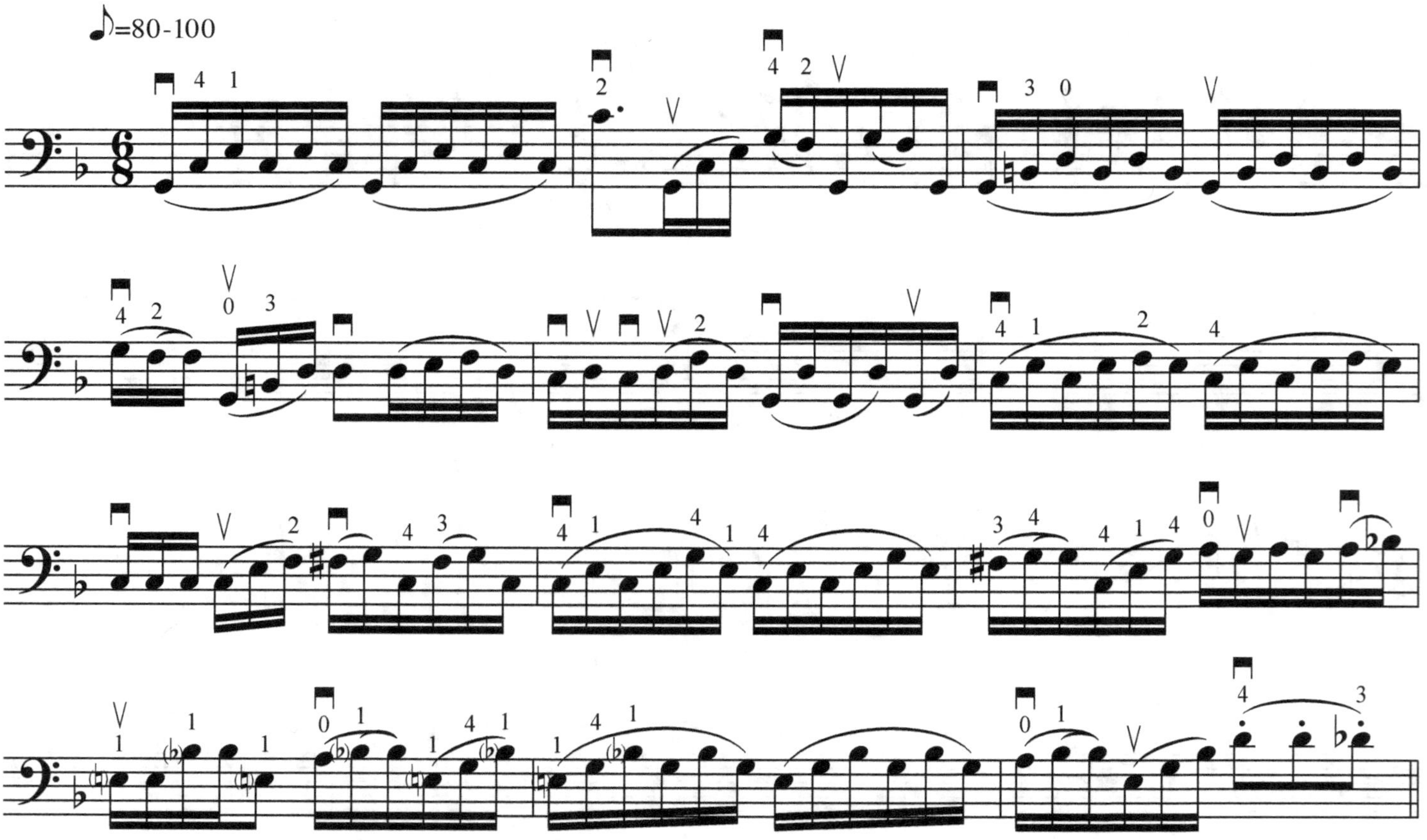

The Romberg Sonata in C Major Study Book for Cello

Bowing: Measures 31-34

Rhythm I: Measures 31-36

Rhythm II: Measures 31-36

©2018 C. Harvey Publications All Rights Reserved.

Optional Advanced Coordination Exercise
Measures 31-36

The + signs mean left-hand pizzicato.

Verbalizing Rhythm
Measures 31-36

In this exercise, the rest is as long as one of the sixteenth notes you play.
1. Say the word "Rest" out loud for all rests.
2. Say the word "Long" out loud when you play all eighth notes.

Fitting the Notes With the Accompaniment
Measures 28-36

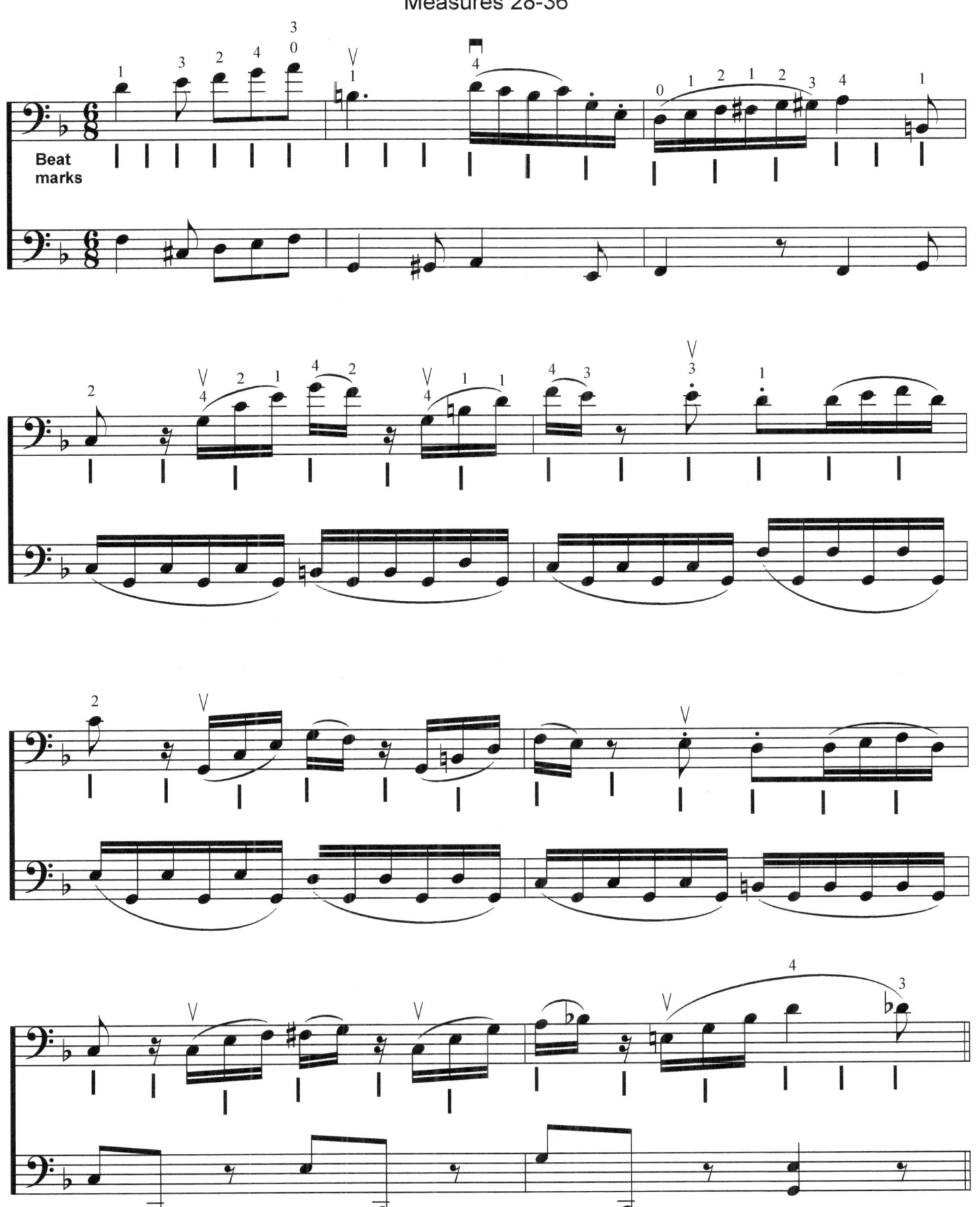

Sonata, Second Movement
Section Four: Measures 37-49

Note: Measures 37-43 are the same as measures 1-7.
Practice the exercises on pages 67-68 to learn those measures.

String Crossing
Measures 43-47

Shifting
Measures 43-49

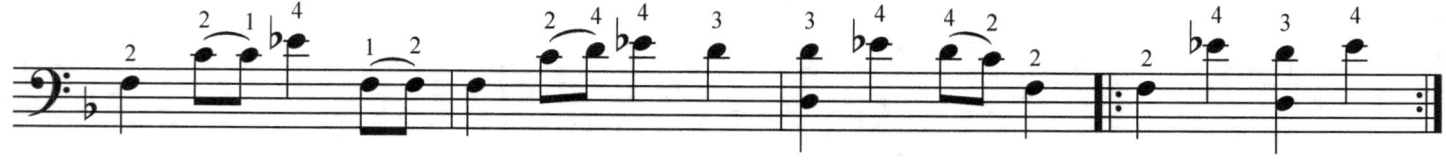

©2018 C. Harvey Publications All Rights Reserved.

Finger Exercise
Measures 43-48

Sonata, Second Movement
Section Five: Measures 50-59 (end)

Learning the Notes
Measures 47-51

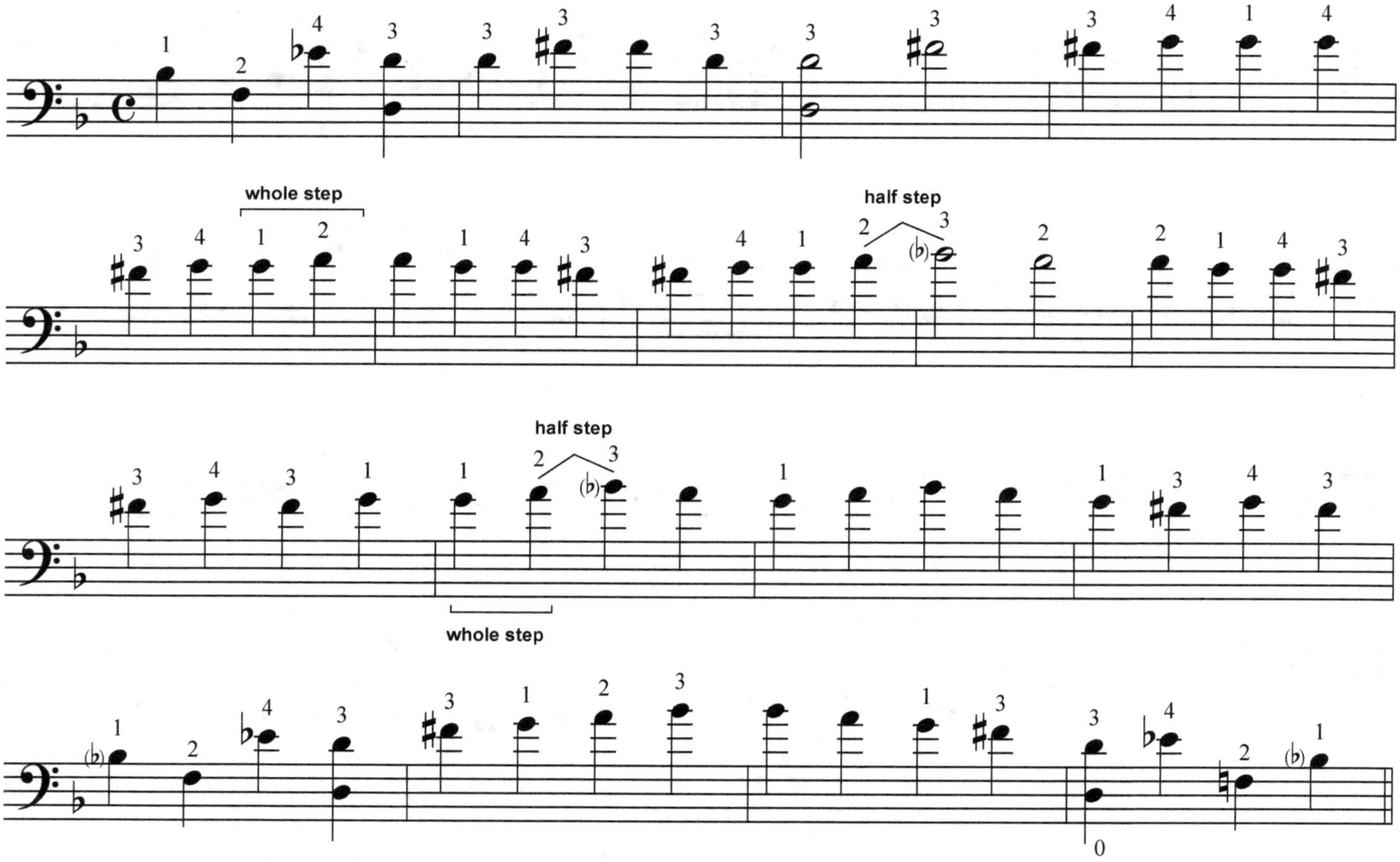

Shifting
Measures 50-59

©2018 C. Harvey Publications All Rights Reserved.

Rhythm
Measures 53-56

Fitting the Notes With the Accompaniment
Measures 53-59

String Crossing
Measures 53-59

Fluency
Measures 51-59

Movement 3: Essential Bowing Exercises

Note: Since the bowing is the trickiest part of playing Movement 3, studying the bowing before working on the actual piece is an efficient way to learn it.

♩=60-90

Play with a light staccato on the eighth notes. The bow may occasionally come off the string for the sixteenths notes if you wish but it is not required.

Bowing No. 1: Measures 1-2, 12-13, 16-17, etc.

Bowing No. 2: Measures 2-5, 166-169

Bowing No. 3: Measures 4-7, 80-83, etc.

©2018 C. Harvey Publications All Rights Reserved.

The Romberg Sonata in C Major Study Book for Cello

89

Bowing No. 4: Measures 8-10, 84-86

Bowing No. 5: Measures 9-12, 166-168

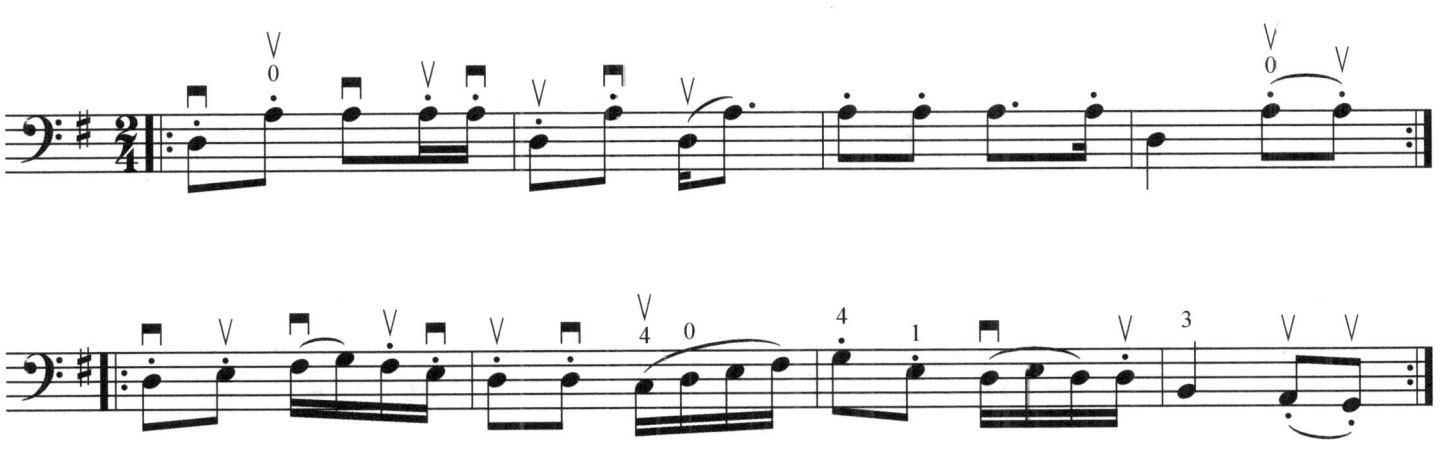

Bowing No. 6: Measures 24-27, 100-103, etc.

©2018 C. Harvey Publications All Rights Reserved.

Bowing No. 7: Measures 31-32

To play this note, think of playing an eighth note but take the bow off the string just before the end of the note so the note is slightly curtailed.

Bowing No. 8: Measures 31-36, 129-133, etc.

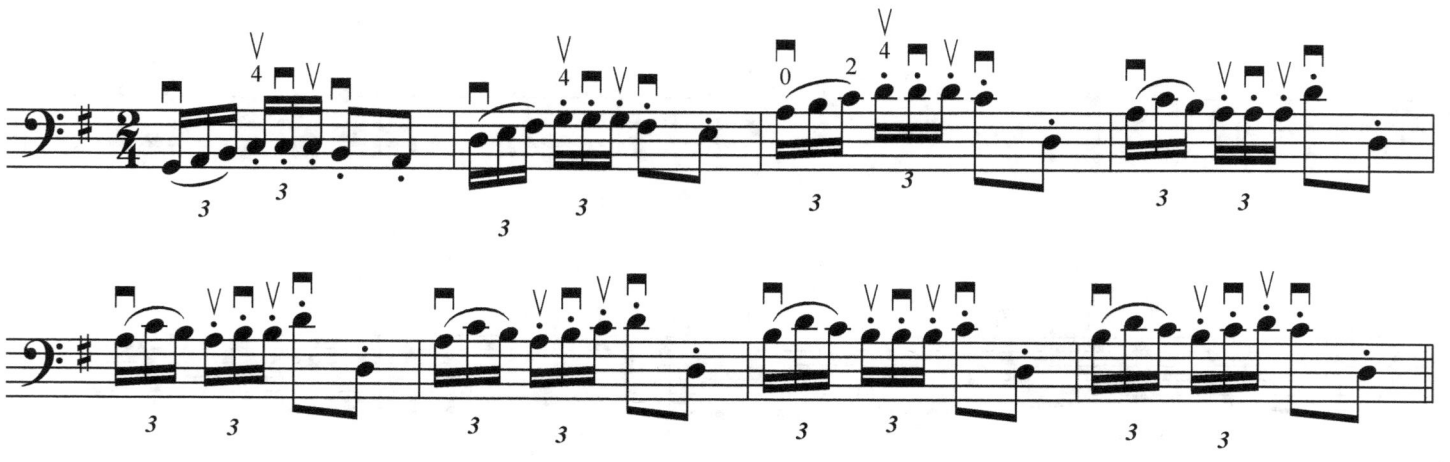

Bowing No. 9: Measures 48-51

Stop your bow gently on the string during the rest and then play the next note, moving the bow in the same direction.

Bowing No. 10: Measures 59, 127

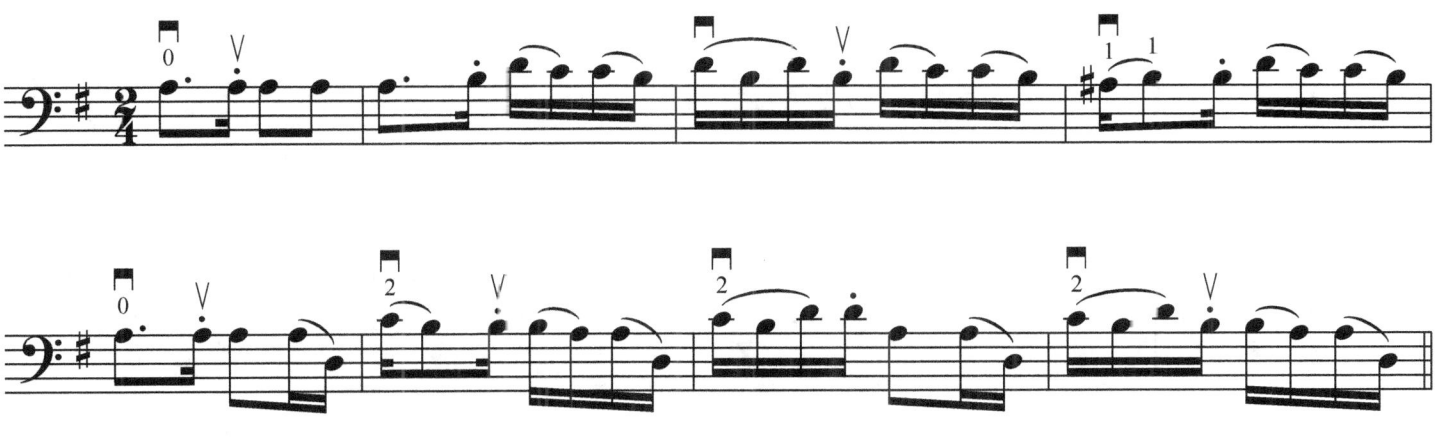

Bowing No. 11: Measures 107-108, 115-116

Bowing No. 12: Measures 122-123

©2018 C. Harvey Publications All Rights Reserved.

Bowing No. 13: Measures 128-129, 179-180

Bowing No. 14: Measures 147-148

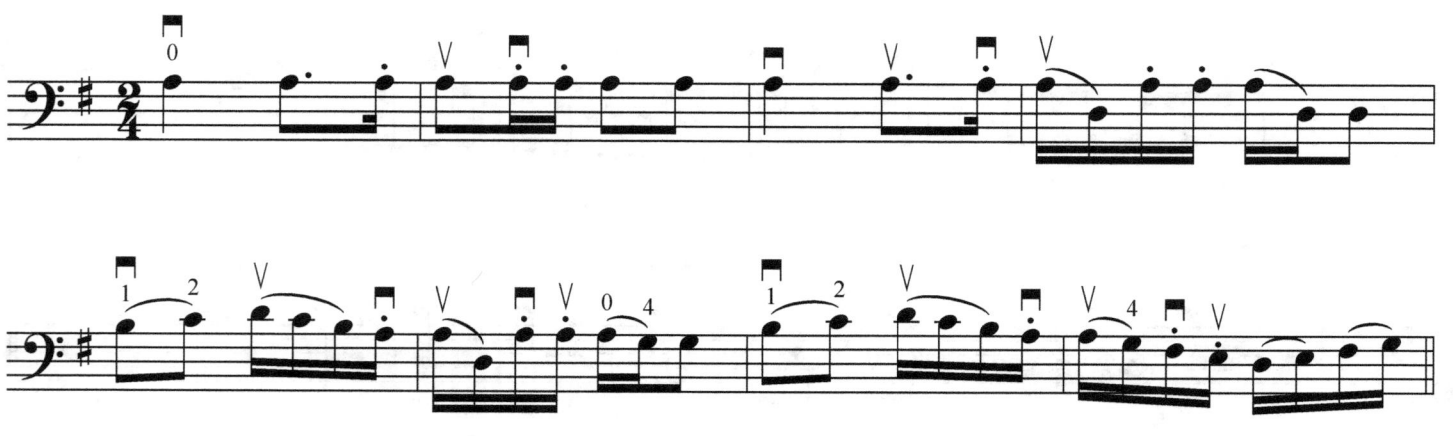

Bowing No. 15: Measures 154-155

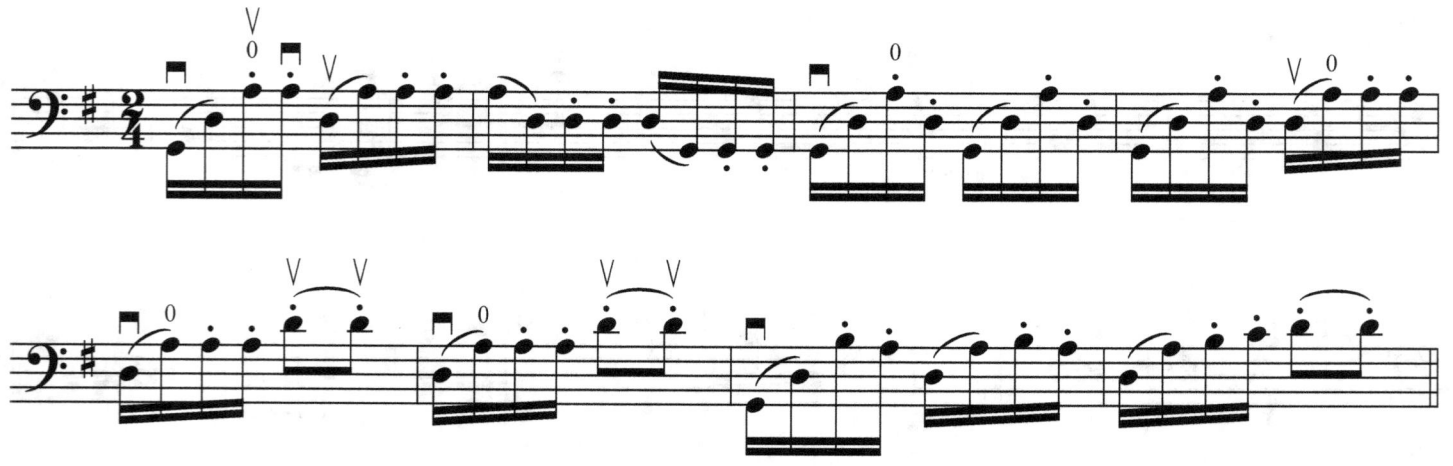

Sonata, Third Movement
Section One: Measures 1-20a

Allegretto

Play with a light staccato on the eighth notes. The bow may occasionally come off the string for the sixteenths notes if you wish but it is not required.

Shifting
Measures 3-4, 13-15, 17-20a

Finger Exercise for Agility
Measures 1-20a

Coordination I
Measures 1-5

The Romberg Sonata in C Major Study Book for Cello

Coordination II
Measures 6-12

Coordination III
Measures 12-20a

©2015 C. Harvey Publications All Rights Reserved.

Sonata, Third Movement
Section Two: Measures 20-42a

Shifting
Measures 25-29

Bowing and Coordination
Measures 20-27

Shifting and Coordination I
Measures 25-26

Shifting and Coordination II
Measures 25-29

The Romberg Sonata in C Major Study Book for Cello

String Crossing and Bow Agility
Measures 30-32

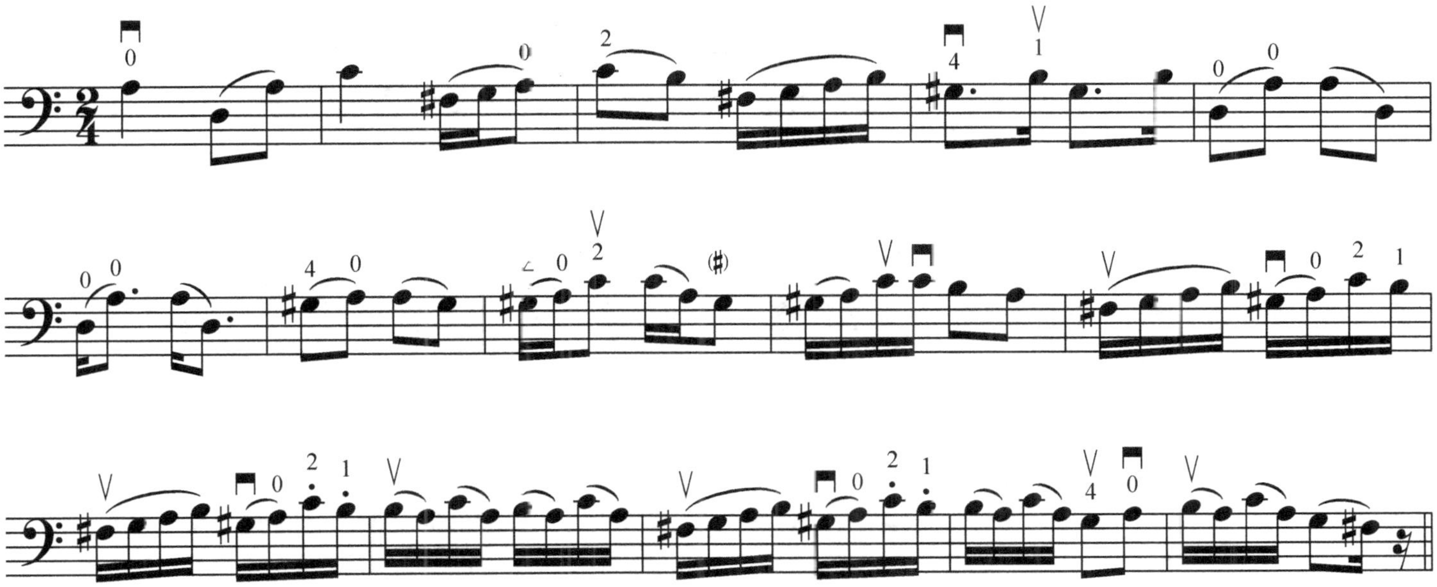

Agility and Bowing
Measures 32-36

©2018 C. Harvey Publications All Rights Reserved.

The Romberg Sonata in C Major Study Book for Cello

Rhythm
Measures 30-37

Shifting: Measures 37-42

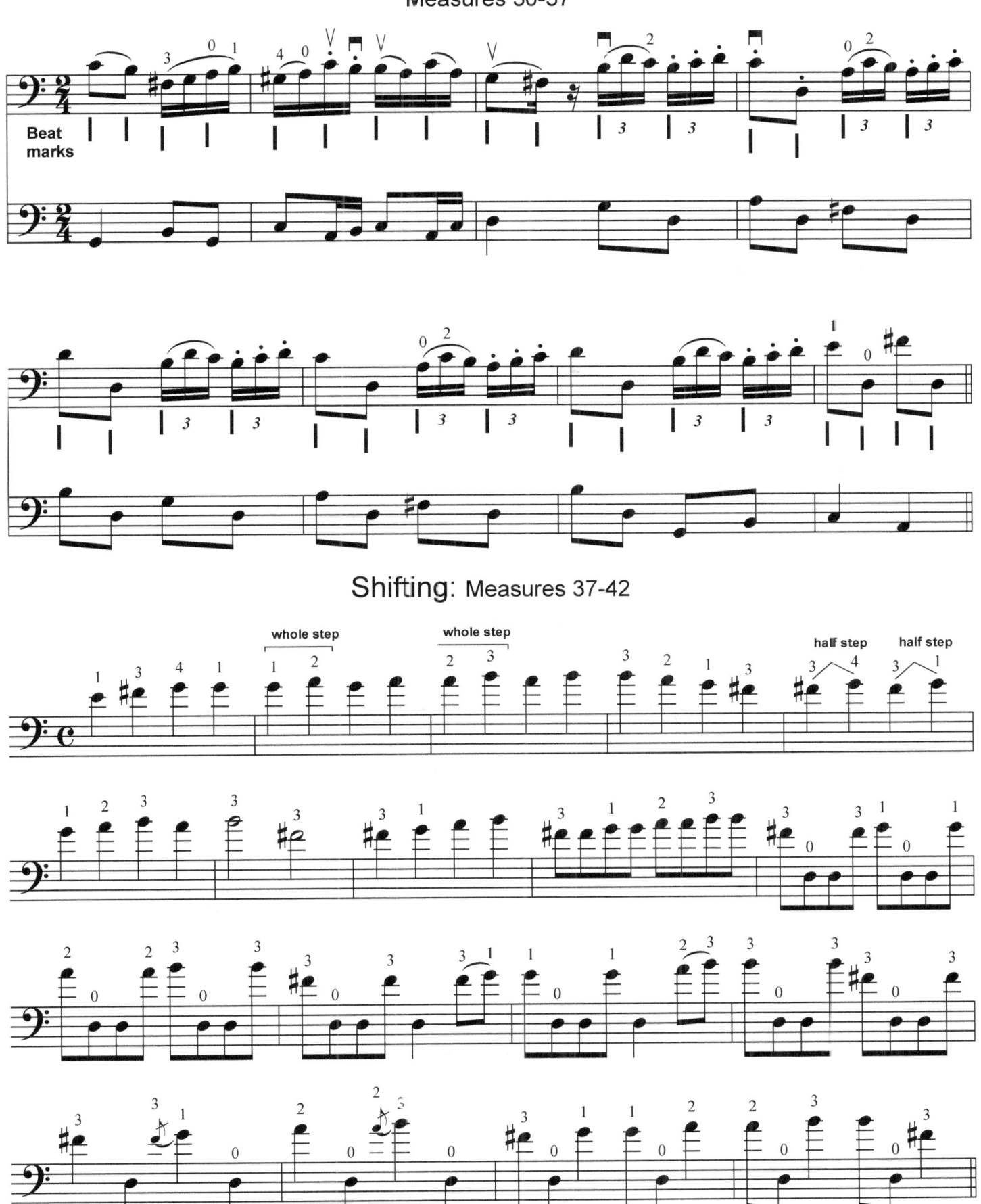

Sonata, Third Movement
Section Three: Measures 42-60a

Rhythm and String Crossing
Measures 42-45

Hold 4th finger down on the string.

Mapping the Positions I
Measures 46-47

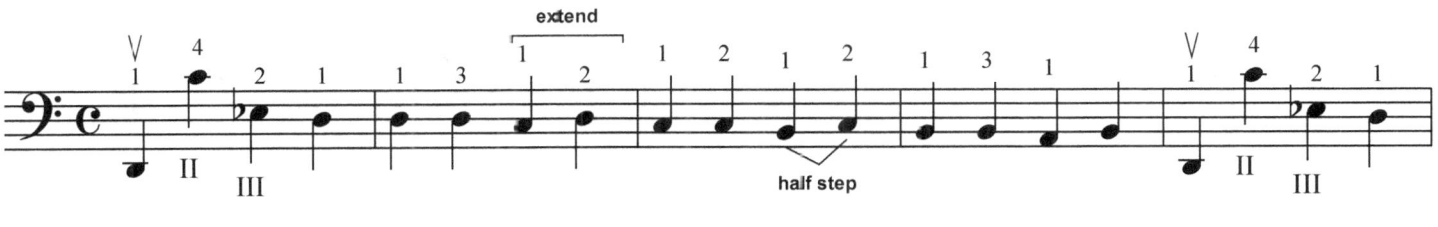

Mapping the Positions II
Measures 46-47

Mapping the Positions III
Measures 46-47

©2018 C. Harvey Publications All Rights Reserved.

Shifting Backwards
Measures 46-47

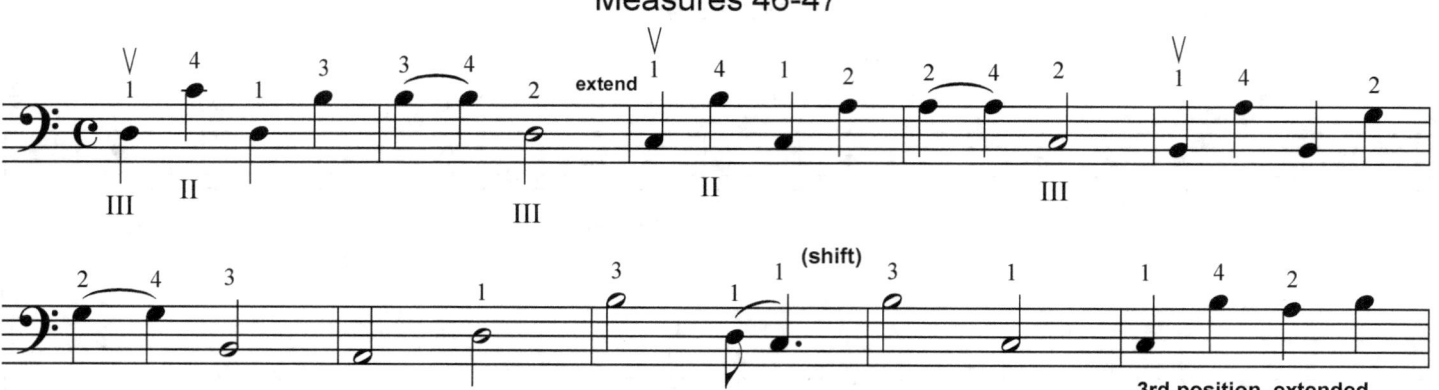

Fluency
Measures 46-47

The Romberg Sonata in C Major Study Book for Cello

Rhythm and Long Bows: Measures 48-52

Shifting: Measures 52-60a

Sonata, Third Movement
Section Four: Measures 60-104a

Learning the Notes I
Measures 60-69

Learning the Notes II
Measures 70-75

**Note: Measures 76-105 are the same as measures 1-27.
Practice the exercises on pages 93-98 to learn those measures.**

Sonata, Third Movement
Section Five: Measures 104-127

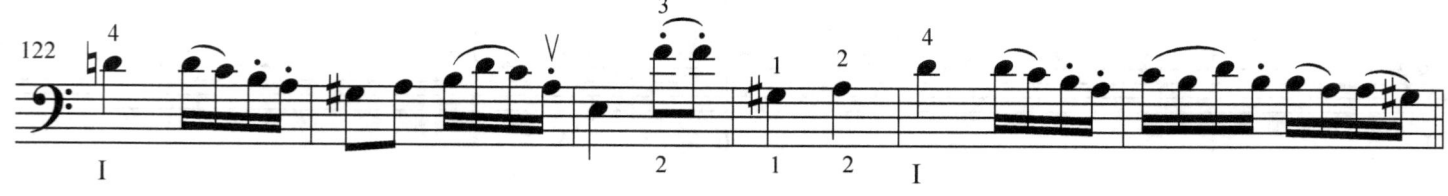

The Romberg Sonata in C Major Study Book for Cello   109

Learning the Notes
Measures 104-107, 112-115

Shifting and Finger Exercise
Measures 104-109

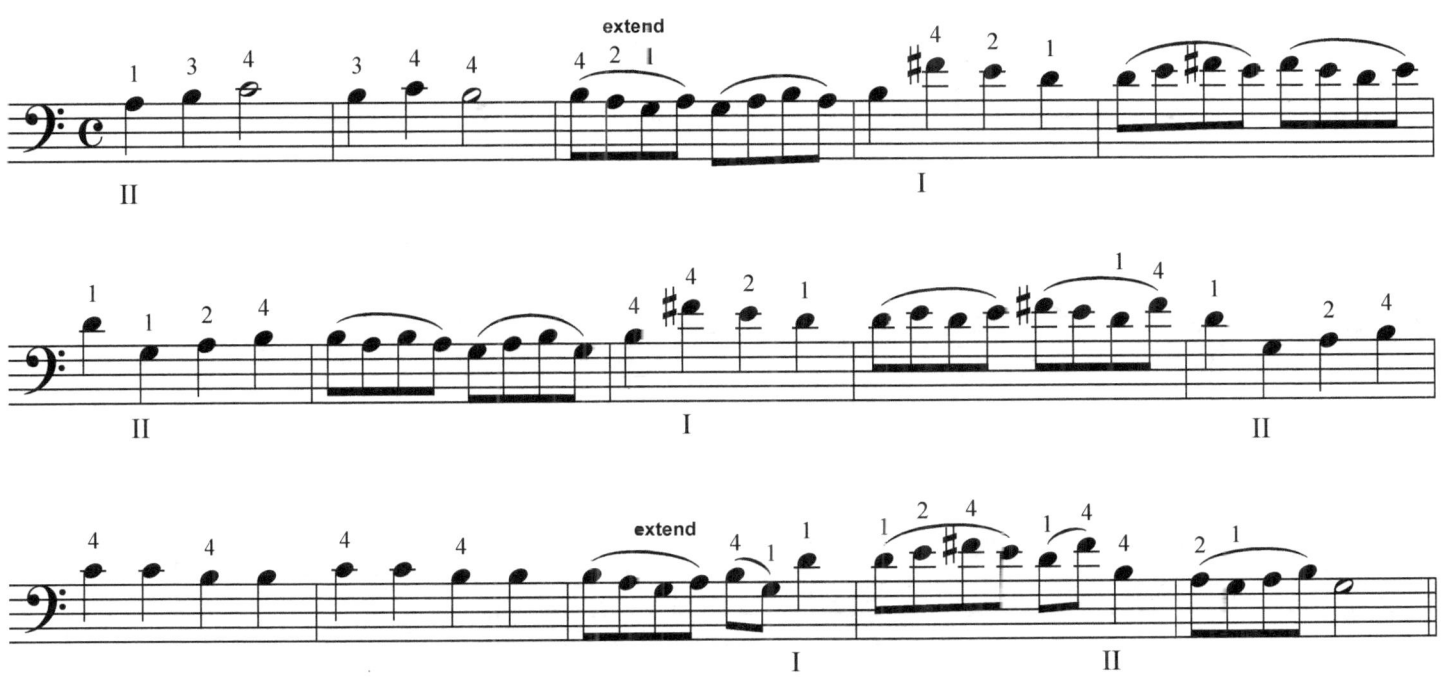

©2018 C. Harvey Publications All Rights Reserved.

Shifting and Reaching Across to the A string
Measures 104-109

Shifting I
Measures 104-119

Shifting II
Measures 111-121

Shifting and Bowing
Measures 111, 119

Learning the Notes
Measures 117-127

Shifting and String Crossing
Measures 124-127

Sonata, Third Movement
Section Six: Measures 128-149a

Bowing II
Measures 128-142

Finger Exercise
Measures 128-142

Spiccato Study
Measures 128-142

Shifting and Bowing
Measures 133-135a

Learning the Notes
Measures 142-149

String Crossing Review
Measures 133-135a

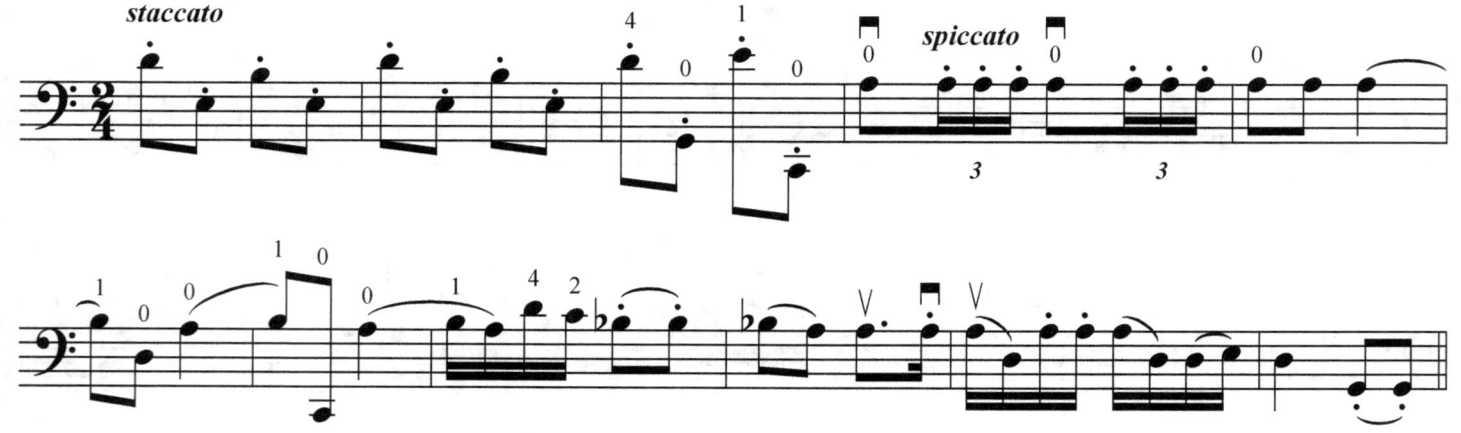

Sonata, Third Movement
Section Seven: Measures 149-178

Shifting
Measures 149-151

Shifting
Measures 150-151, 155-160

Double Stops for Intonation
Measures 149-159

Learning the Notes: Measures 159-164

Note: Measures 165-173 are the same as measures 1-8.
Practice the exercises on pages 93-95 to learn those measures.

Shifting and Bowing: Measures 174-178

Sonata, Third Movement
Section Eight: Measures 179-207 (end)

Shifting
Measures 180-185

Finger and Bow Exercise: Measures 179-185

Left and Right Hand Agility
Measures 179-183, 187-191

Shifting During Open Strings I
Measures 180-183, 187-191

Shifting During Open Strings II
Measures 184-185

Shifting During Open Strings III
Measures 192-193

Shifting During Open Strings IV
Measures 180-193

Fluency
Measures 180-194

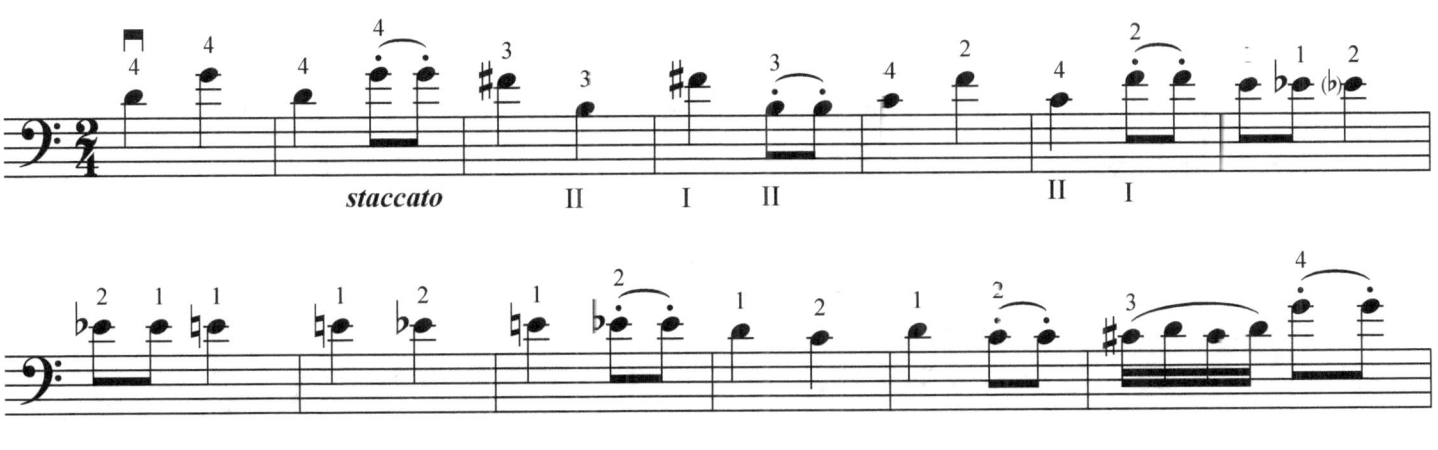

Learning the Notes
Measures 193-200

Finger Exercise
Measures 200-207

Bowing
Measures 200-207

Sonata

Allegro

The Romberg Sonata in C Major Study Book for Cello

The Romberg Sonata in C Major Study Book for Cello

The Romberg Sonata in C Major Study Book for Cello

The Romberg Sonata in C Major Study Book for Cello

Allegretto

The Romberg Sonata in C Major Study Book for Cello 135

The Romberg Sonata in C Major Study Book for Cello 137

Was this book helpful?
We would love it if you left a review where you bought it!

Not so helpful?
We're happy to hear any feedback. Was the book what you expected from what we described? If not, let us know how we can describe it better. Or, let us know how the book could be more helpful to you. Just send an email with your comments or questions to info@charveypublications.com.

Many more cello study books and duets are available at
www.charveypublications.com.

Downloadable study books and duets are available at
www.learnstrings.com.

Don't see what you need?
Send us an email suggesting a book: info@charveypublications.com. While we regret that we cannot write a book for every suggestion, we do use customer feedback to help determine which books to publish next. Some of our most popular books were written in response to customer suggestions!

available from **www.charveypublications.com**: CHP332
The Bach Cello Suite No. 1 Study Book

Note: The Suite is broken up into sections in this study book. The complete Suite is at the back of the book.

Suite No. 1: Prelude
Part One: Measures 1-4 (Bowing #1)

Suite by J. S. Bach
Exercises by Cassia Harvey

Double Stops for Intonation
Measures 1-4

©2017 C. Harvey Publications All Rights Reserved.

www.ingramcontent.com/pod-product-compliance
Lightning Source LLC
Chambersburg PA
CBHW051414070526
44584CB00023B/3426